The DESERT BLOOMS

The DESERT BLOOMS

*A personal adventure
in growing old creatively*

SARAH-PATTON BOYLE

Abingdon Press
Nashville

The Desert Blooms

A Personal Adventure in Growing Old Creatively
Copyright © 1983 by Sarah-Patton Boyle

Third Printing 1986

Library of Congress Cataloging in Publication Data

BOYLE, SARAH-PATTON.
  The desert blooms.
    1. Boyle, Sarah-Patton. 2. Aged women—United States—Biography. 3. Creative ability. 4. Life style. I. Title.
HQ1413.B68A33   1983   305.2'6'0924   83-8800

ISBN 0-687-10484-X

Scripture quotations in this publication unless otherwise noted (or Scripture quotations noted RSV) are from the Revised Standard Version of the Bible, copyrighted 1946, 1952, © 1971, 1973 by the Division of Christian Education of the National Council of the Churches of Christ in the U.S.A., and are used by permission.

MANUFACTURED BY THE PARTHENON PRESS AT
NASHVILLE, TENNESSEE, UNITED STATES OF AMERICA

To Stringfellow Barr,
who made me feel fully human when I was less than seven,
and Jim Munroe, who made me feel fully human
when I was more than seventy, this book
is gratefully dedicated.

ACKNOWLEDGMENTS

It is a pleasure to express appreciation to the following institutions and persons:

Trinity Episcopal Church, which gracefully combines respect for personal freedom with patient acceptance of human peculiarities and is eager to help anyone whenever help is sought. I am especially grateful to Jerry Riley, the rector, for the variety of the excellent church classes and activities, and for his interest and encouragement as I wrote this book. That kind of support from the church and the rector made writing far easier.

The administrators and staff of Goodwin House for presenting a model of courtesy, kindness, and creativity in a well-run community for retired people. Without their good care of my cousin Stringfellow Barr (Frank), I could not have survived the experience described in chapter 22.

The Arlington County Recreation Division and Adult Education programs that taught me the knowledge and skills to launch into a new life when I was old.

Columbia Baptist Church, where I attended classes

and groups that focused on self-understanding and outreach. Instructed by Dr. H. Dale Keeton, their skillful minister of counseling, and sustained by Ruth Ann Barr and their other cordial group members and staff, I learned much about turning ordeals into adventures.

The American Association of Retired Persons for supplying through their publications clues to some needed solutions.

The Gray Panthers for substantial encouragement and support when I most needed it. Especially, I'm indebted to Oregon's champion Gray Panther, Ruth Haefner, who has long been my booster, backer, catalyst, and friend.

Chad Walsh, who gently hounded me to produce this book.

Jim Munroe, who can point out one hundred needed improvements and still leave an author feeling that the manuscript is good.

Dr. John F. Woolverton for valuable critical analysis.

Jean Trakowski, for her brilliant ministry of applause.

Dora Shaw, whose courage, independence, and brave struggle to enjoy life proclaimed that a stout spirit is stronger than any handicap.

George Fleming, rector of St. Paul's, Bailey's Crossroads, who by endless self-giving offers impressive lessons in faithful service.

Dr. Kenneth W. Berger, my internist, for keeping me healthier and more joyfully active than many younger people.

Gordon and Mary Cosby for their creative steadfastness, Ellen Campbell for her loving search, Scarlett Makielski for her spiritual insights and support, Frances Stebbins for her encouragement and criticism, and Jessica Feingold for her timely feedback.

The following persons have helped me in various ways—by typing or commenting on my manuscript, by correcting my incredible spelling, by offering cogent suggestions, needed information, special points of view, or clues for contending:

Janet Tulloch, T. J. Sellers, Charles Stebbins, Beth Tucker, Don and Cindy Seils, Primrose Vining, Shelley Stasny, Baylor Cromwell, Carol Menne, Alicia Flynn, Bill Royal, Janet Riley, and Sadie Finkel.

Finally and especially, Frieda Jenkinson, who died suddenly before this book went to press. During the four years I knew her, Frieda helped me in so many ways that I called her "my staff."

Many others have contributed briefly but effectively. I am grateful to them, although they are too numerous to mention by name.

C O N T E N T S

This book is a simple, striptease account of my own experience with aging.

It begins with my naive optimism concerning my ability to cope, when in my sixtieth year, I moved from a small town to a teeming suburb of Washington, D.C. There, seen as just another gray-haired woman, my individual identity was lost. Each person reacted to me according to his or her stereotype of old age.

That sudden experience of being stereotyped drove away my cheerful expectations. Then came bewilderment, struggle, rebellion, and despair. Finally, I moved into a new understanding of myself, my world, my faith, and—at last—into hard-fought-for fulfillment.

I do not deal with grinding poverty or enervating ill health, real as they often are in old age. For I have not suffered them. I focus on psychological pressures that come with aging in a rapidly changing, youth-oriented culture.

My purpose in writing the book is to help older readers understand their experiences, revive their wilting self-images, and spark their coping skills. In younger readers, I want to reduce fear of aging by showing that vigor, adventures of the mind and spirit, and inner triumph are possible at any age. In all readers, I seek to increase awareness of the unintentionally dehumanizing messages that are continually sent us as we grow older. And in all, I strive to confirm the truth that ultimate solutions are spiritually based.

I do not pretend to speak for all old people. I proclaim that old people are simply people who are old. (Although some people dislike my free use of the word "old," I think that using euphemisms implies that old age is shameful.) I can speak for the old only by asserting that any universal human need is theirs. An urgent need of every human being is to be related to as an individual, not as a faceless member of some group.

Conversations and incidents in the book are factual, not invented. For greater clarity or brevity, I sometimes attribute to one person comments and behavior actually gathered from more than one. For instance, the person I call the Rev. Joseph Lox is composite. But all that I attribute to him was indeed said or done in my presence by some clergymen of his persuasion. My account of experiences with his church combines encounters I had in three churches, none named St. Luke's.

Except for this kind of rearrangement, the story almost photographically describes scenes that really happened. Some of the people mentioned in the book (or persons authorized to speak for them) graciously consented to have their real names used. This is true of the characters in chapter 24 except for the man I call Tom, who preferred anonymity. Except where permission to use a real name was granted, all names throughout the book have been changed and often physical desriptions as well.

Even though I agonized over many of the encounters I describe, I can honestly say now that the experience of growing old is one I deeply value. In a letter addressed to Jessica Feingold (previously with the Jewish Theological Seminary of America) and written before I started writing this book, I said:

"It's all very fascinating as well as being painful. It's like exploring a new country full of new sights, new problems, new dangers, and in which one can't communicate very well and must learn a new language. I get homesick sometimes for life as I once knew it. And yet I'm beginning to feel that if I could get a ticket home, I would want it to be round-trip. This land is becoming my land."

PART I

The Shock of Discovery

1

"Plow in Hope"

I am seventy-seven years old. Some of the last thirteen years have been the happiest of my life. I will not say, "Old age is the golden age." It's seldom that easy. But it may be a kind of gold mine since gold can be found there if we search and dig.

I also think of old age as a time when ripe plums drop less often in our laps. We have to climb the tree to get them. But climbing can be fun. It keeps us in condition. And the plums are worth it. When people ask my secret of a happy old age, I answer that it's the grace of God mediated through determination, persistence, and hard work—on myself.

Eighteen years ago I faced the fact that the life I had known was over. I had lost my husband. My children were far away, intent on finding mates and creating careers. The Southern civil rights revolution of the 1950s, which had riveted my attention and drained my energies for fifteen years, had changed direction and was moving swiftly away from my area of competence and commitment. Like many another woman my age whose family is gone and whose job, if she had one, "doesn't need her anymore," I was like a clipped blossom—one day dancing on its bush, the next severed and thrust into a slim vase. The blossom's identity is still there is a sense, yet it is separated from all that was responsible for that identity.

If there was anything unusual about my situation, it was that I lacked the sense to be frightened. It never crossed my mind to think of myself as a cut and fading flower. I assumed that I was a growing plant about to be transplanted into new ground. I knew what I wanted from the rest of my life. I wanted to bring into full function the person I had been created to be. I saw no great obstacles. I believed that a plan for my life existed and that I was moving toward its fulfillment.

In my almost sixty years I had learned, like Edison, many things that wouldn't work and even a few that would. I was resolved to make adventures out of any ordeals I met, a skill I learned during the civil rights revolution when I was often under attack. Within myself I felt the strong outward thrust of accumulated wisdom and practical know-how. I expected to reap a good harvest by using them. A future was out there waiting. It didn't occur to me that I might not be able to deal with it.

Nothing ahead could be worse than the ordeals I had already weathered, I thought. Hadn't I even survived my husband's sudden announcement that when the last of our children left home, he would leave too? True, I had been shocked and bitterly hurt. But after a period of bewildered pain, I agreed that our marriage had become an empty shell. The closeness we had shared during our first sixteen years had steadily eroded until we were only friendly strangers—although I suspected that we got along as well as most couples our age. I had thought that when just the two of us were home, we might draw closer again. He thought differently, however. So when all my protests were expressed, I consented to the separation without ill will.

There were some positive elements in the situation. As is true of many people, I felt inside me the steady pressure of an unlived life, of unfulfilled potential, of unsatisfied areas in my being. Family responsibilities had elbowed my more personal yearnings aside. But now, with my tasks as homemaker finished, I could hurl the full force of my matured experience and broadened vision into expressing my whole self.

I would decorate my home exactly as I wanted it, without having my favorite choices vetoed by someone with an equal right to determine how our home looked. Uninterrupted, I could work on my writing each day as long as the words poured freely. When nothing more pressed up from within, I could grab an apple, banana or hunk of cheese, gulp it down, and collapse on my bed for restoring sleep—regardless of the time of day. And I could paint pictures all day when the mood seized me, without ever having to shatter the spell by dashing out for groceries, fixing dinner, or retrieving garments before the cleaners closed.

Moreover, without having to wonder if my husband would feel embarrassed or left out by my conglomerate selections, I could gather round me people who appealed to me for strange reasons or for no identifiable reasons. I would spend no more hours entertaining other people's friends. In short, I could be me! Just me, every minute of every day, without having to be considerate of, or accountable to, other persons on whose lives mine impinged.

I could do what I wanted when I wanted to. I could

spend money as I saw fit, without having to explain or justify. I could take all the surging yearnings and whims that were part of me and do with them as my whole nature, and mine alone, prescribed.

If all this sounds as if I spent thirty-three years of marriage seething with rebellion against household drudgery, let me correct that impression. While it lasted, the homemaker's role brought me much satisfaction. I enjoyed and was grateful for the biological and human roles of wife and mother. I liked taking care of people, and I felt good about taking care of my family.

But there were costs, even when I gladly paid them. By nature I am highly individual and independent. My unlived life had beckoned often and the thought had occurred to me now and then that nothing held me back but a ball and chain. So now that liberty was thrust unsought upon me, I resolved to focus, not on what I had lost, but on what I would gain.

I decided to leave the college town where I lived and move near the nation's capital, where there were opportunities to build any kind of life I wanted. I sold my house in Charlottesville, Virginia, and went.

As I approached my destination, gentle landscapes of hills and meadows, forests and streams were replaced by man-made eyesores: a city dump, half-jagged, half-limp, steam shovels gouging great holes in hillsides; service stations, buildings under construction, and cloverleaf intersections. Finally I reached the garden apartment complex where I had secured my new home.

Moving from a town in the foothills of the mountains to the outskirts of a burgeoning great city can be instantly depressing. And while Washington proper is beautiful, rapid growth in its surrounding territory has inevitably left a painful mark. But so steeped was I in the landscapes with which I had lived that it was several months before the ugliness broke through my memories of surrounding beauty and oppressed my consciousness. At first I just noted the eyesores and let them pass.

I got my key from a friendly girl in the office and went to my apartment to await my furniture. The temperature was in the nineties and as I opened my door, the chemical odor of fresh paint swept out on a wave of warm air. Moving quickly to the windows, I tugged at sticking sashes until most of them came up. The air that rushed in was hardly cooler than the heavy vapor inside, but at least it moved. My eyes circled bare walls, bare floors, bare windows. I ignored the dismal symbolism and the uneasy feelings it triggered. Sitting on my bedroom windowsill, I said aloud briskly, "When my stuff comes, this place will become a home." Then I glanced below. An asphalt parking lot stretched out, littered with reminders of our throw-away culture, sweltering and gray.

Quickly I raised my eyes to window level and looked with relief into a big oak tree. Its long branches reached above and to both sides of my large double window, giving me a feeling of being almost in a tree house. Every window in this apartment, even the bathroom, looked into some kind of tree. It was chiefly this fact, plus its low rent, that had induced me to take it. Even better than my bedroom oak was the huge dogwood that embraced all three south windows in my living room. Each spring that dogwood would delight my eyes with its billows of white bloom. Each fall it would hold out piercingly crimson and scarlet leaves.

Trees say something I like to hear about the nature of the universe. I studied my bedroom oak, noting how fearfully and wonderfully all trees are made. Every segment of their bark is different from every other segment, yet rhythmic with the rest. No two leaves on any tree are quite the same, but all clearly belong together. Each limb sways in its own way, yet is joined to the trunk. Birds rest in trees, each bird uniquely itself, singing its own song, yet united with all others of its kind across thousands of miles and years by the patterns of its species.

Because I believe that life is created as a unified whole, I had a sense, that first day, of being accepted by the very heart of the universe. I was at home in the creation, content to be part of it. We belonged to each other, and this sense of belonging made me feel secure in my new life. I saw my past as having moved me toward the fulfillment of my destiny. I was certain that my most productive years lay ahead. It was as though all that had happened was only the first two acts in a significant drama. Act three was about to begin. As the curtain rose, I was full of suspense.

Looking toward the future, I saw it hung with golden mist. My mind acknowledged the fact that problems, frustrations, and disappointments are a standard ingredient in every situation. But my heart had traffic only with utopia. I saw myself triumphant over all ills. I liked to grapple with obstacles. Grappling tones us up emotionally and spiritually, just as muscles and blood vessels are toned up with vigorous exercise. I wanted to be strong and limber through and through. And I knew that only frequent tussles with hard realities maintain strength and limberness in all parts of our being. I didn't expect to be problem-free. But I had not expected problems I couldn't handle. I always had believed that where there is a difficulty, there is a way out. So I felt a minimum of anxiety about my new life.

The trouble was that the surprises, challenges, and testing I actually met were much more radical than anticipated. They struck at the root of my capacity to relate to others and to contend with challenges and testing. They undercut my ability to fight back, even my belief that I could. As a result, the chief characteristics I had taken for granted in myself—my creativity and my joy in others—steadily withered like foliage in a drought.

2

Shallow Grooves

For several months my days were full of interest and new experience. So busy was I
savoring freedom and adventure that empty places in
me were only dimly felt. I was like a jack-in-the-box
whose hooked-down top is suddenly released. My
upward leap from confinement was all-consuming.

I explored short cuts, shopping centers, fabric
shops, book shops, art galleries, libraries, parks,
churches. I rejoiced in the tiny challenges and
triumphs these investigations brought. Each night I
was pleasantly weary, satisfied with the day's accomplishment, and grateful.

But when my apartment was decorated and my
other preparations made, and I was ready to start
living my new life, an unnerving discovery slugged
me. My luxurious sense of freedom to do what I
chose when I chose was gone! Far from plunging
eagerly into painting and writing, as I had expected, I
felt immobilized.

How could this be? It didn't make sense! Now I had
time for all the things I had fretted to do when I didn't
have time. For the first time in my life, conditions were
absolutely right for full-scale creativity!

Or were they? Something in me seemed to cry out that I had been taken off my hinges. Like a door freed from its restricting connections with the frame, far from at last being able to swing in all directions at will, I could only lean stiffly against the wall. I saw that I actually needed the rigid structuring my demanding former roles had imposed! Without it a new tyrant seized me. Free to do anything any time, I must choose what I would do and not do in each moment of every day! I sagged under the weight of countless petty decisions.

When should I rise, bathe, eat, shop, exercise, tidy the apartment? When should I write, paint, seek out friends? These matters had been determined in my old life—some by well-established routines, others by the fact that I had to instantly grasp any chance to do my own thing. Under pressure from family emergencies and from time that was always too short, I had executed tasks as they came to hand, without pausing for questions or internal debate. Now, every hour was choked with alternatives. Moreover, now that all pursuits were of my own choosing, there seemed no longer a way to escape into freedom, or any territory designated free.

With no impetus from outside pressures to push me into action, not only did every move involve a decision, it also involved a deliberate act of will! I found this curiously exhausting. Actions that throughout my life had been almost automatic, now seemed not worth the effort they required. Even letter writing ceased to be a pleasure and became a chore.

As a last straw, rationalization reared its head. Instead of working at painting or writing, I cunningly assured myself that I should take a long walk on such a lovely day, or that I should read some new book to keep me up with the times. Why not? Didn't I have the rest of that day and tomorrow and all the days thereafter to get my creative work done? Why all the rush?

Appalled, I reassessed my situation. I had not suspected that freedom from responsibility might impede my creativity more than overwork and a tight schedule. It had not occurred to me to be grateful for the encroachments of family life. For family sharing, family presence in the background, family companionship (what there was of it in our rush-rush era) I had been grateful. But I had not been grateful for the impingement of other lives that had forced me in prescribed directions. I never suspected that the pushing and pulling of other people had carried me easily, as in a current. I had thought I did all the carrying.

How difficult it is, I suddenly realized, for us feeble mortals to function in shallow grooves! In the past, I had looked down on routines and habits as poor substitutes for spontaneity and obvious deterrents to it. But with my routines and habits taken away, I was forced to admit they were essential to my spontaneity. In my old life, I woke each morning with the day's activities mostly settled by the fixed demands of my roles. My energy and attention were thereby freed for simply getting my tasks done. I slipped easily along grooves of routines and habits worn so deep and smooth that little effort was needed. And when my boring chores were done, I had stored up vitality to use as I pleased. I could leap into creativity at every chance, like a released spring.

I recalled with embarrassment having smugly assumed during the first weeks of my new freedom that so-called retirement shock was just the drawing back of timid, unimaginative souls from anything new. I had felt no empathy with sad-faced retirees who complained of having been uprooted from work that made life worthwhile. Why call it uprooted? I called it transplanted!

But now that the honeymoon of my new life was over, I had to admit that uprooted was how I felt. It was clear that some form of retirement shock had hit me, and that it was not a malady with an easy cure. To find a cure, I must work hard and possibly for a very long time. And it was time to start.

I assumed I would succeed. "Where there's a problem, there's a solution," I reminded myself firmly. I would net nothing by brooding philosophically on my discovery that freedom is not what it's cracked up to be. I must begin with what I had learned about myself—that I needed structure and familiar routines even more than I needed freedom. I must develop a new structure, and new routines that would become grooves as smooth and deep as the old ones. But that called for discipline!

I sat down and made a schedule. When finished, it looked like one a youngster might be handed at boarding school, or an adult at a weekend conference. There were designated times for work, recreation, rest and free periods.

Being an early riser, I must begin the morning with devotions at six. Then would come breakfast, grooming, office hours, housework, shopping, errands, exercise, fellowship, and any extras—pleasant or unpleasant—I wished to add. In following such a schedule, I hoped to lose my feelings of limbo and to regain a sense of standing on firm ground. But I must allow enough flexibility for freedom without losing the firm support of discipline. Devotions, work, and people were the only big musts that could not be omitted.

Devotions would include Bible study, inspirational reading, prayer and meditation. I had long enjoyed them all with frequency, though not with regularity. I had prayed every day, but not at the same time. I read the Bible often but not every day. I kept bedside devotional books that I sometimes read at night. I had resisted the idea of regularity, thinking it mechanical and therefore meaningless. The spiritual life above all, I claimed, should be spontaneous.

Wiser now, I saw that if I had established spiritual routines, my present life would not be devoid of familiar grooves. I would have a comfortable, supporting structure from which to deal with the drastic changes and dislocations I had met. Spiritual routines can be followed continuously from childhood through old age. Largely independent of both circumstances and human relationships, they are almost indestructible from outside. They ensure an enduring nucleus to sustain us under all conditions. Secure in them we can cope successfully with outer destruction. Establishing spiritual grooves in which to relax and gather strength may well be the greatest need of our day.

In my new schedule, after devotions, breakfast and grooming, I must go to my desk at eight o'clock sharp and work until noon, regardless of how I felt. I could work longer if I wished, but not less. There would be no I'm–not–in–the–mood–for–writing–today excuses. My hours at my typewriter must be taken as seriously if I were an employee in an office. Only real illnesses and emergencies would be acceptable excuses for absences, tardiness or early departure. I would regard writing as my job, painting as my hobby. That meant I could use painting time for writing when I wished, but not the other way around.

Afternoons and evenings were more flexible than mornings. Prescribed activities could be shortened, moved to a different time or even occasionally skipped. The important thing was to follow the schedule closely, unless there was a good reason for not doing it.

I should do some housework each afternoon even if there seemed no need. When living alone, it's too easy to let our standard go down and down until our home looks OK to us but grisly to a visitor. Each day I should also do something that challenged my mind. For minds, like hearts, won't stay the same. If they don't grow, they shrink.

Following my schedule brought back some of my old feeling that there was free territory to retreat to. Once more there was something to rebel against and escape from when my inner tensions rose! How much that I had believed harmful had in fact been used to fill my needs! I hoped I would not again hastily reject frustrating circumstances, but would instead look for ways to use them.

Some time each day, short or long, must be spent interacting with people, I decided. Human interaction is essential for emotional and spiritual health, just as exercise is essential for physical health. A tendency to withdraw is a grave danger when we live alone, and I had already seen warning signs. More than once when I could have asked a friend to dinner, I caught myself opting for a visit to a movie alone. No more of that!

When friends weren't available, I must attend a lecture or a civic or religious meeting where audience participation was invited. Eventually, from notices, announcements, and calls of inquiry I made to church offices and chairmen of organizations, I made a file of such meetings that met regularly. By flipping through this file on almost any day I could find some group to join for interaction and exchange.

Open meetings of Alcoholics Anonymous, at which nonmembers are always welcome, were high on my list. Their recovery program is so broad and sound that it can be applied not just to problem-drinking but to almost any personal problem. Later, when my own accumulating distresses overwhelmed me, I leaned heavily on what I had learned from AA.

When no groups were available, my schedule suggested that I go to the nearest shopping center, and spend an hour milling around stores, watching for chances to make pleasant remarks to clerks and customers. This practice can be a fine art. I had learned it from my mother and grandmother, who passed it on to me as part of their rural heritage. As I recaptured it, I noted how many pleasant comments can be made sincerely to strangers. "You know, your hair-do is just lovely. Where did you have it done?" "Just now I watched you selecting your fruits and vegetables, and I'm impressed by how much you seem to know about it." "I've been admiring your attractive sandals." Or to a clerk, "I can't help noticing what careful attention you give your customers."

Sometimes I could see in the person's eyes that my tiny gesture brought real pleasure. Once a woman reached out impulsively and pressed my hand. "You know, that's the first nice thing anyone has said to me today. Thank you. I needed it." Sometimes an eager response showed me that the person wanted interaction as much as I. On two occasions, a little seed of appreciation later grew into a rewarding relationship.

In the years since then, I have developed better ways to achieve human interaction when I need it. But it's worth noting that even these early, sometimes awkward, efforts were more effective than one might think. They served my needs at the time and also helped me develop skills in noticing people's assets and in offering positive reinforcement. All this helped me later, as I struggled against forces that seemed bent on unplugging me from the human race.

3

Who Am I?

The hardest part of establishing my new disciplines was making myself perform boring routines when no one was served by my doing them and there was no one to blame for my having to do them! I was unprepared for the dreariness of necessary housekeeping done for myself alone. I had to learn that not just other people but life itself forces upon us certain built-in drudgeries.

My housework—both the part I liked and the part I hated—had always been done for someone else. As a child, I had performed my little chores to please and to help my mother. Later, I had labored to give my husband an acceptable home and to take good care of our children. I had been aware that the dimension of loving service somewhat redeemed these treadmill routines. But the full extent of that dimension escaped me until I had to do them without it. Scrubbing, vacuuming, dusting, waxing, bed changing, dish and window washing still had to be done. And now their flatness and meaninglessness was terrible and new.

Moreover, as I moved through my first year on my own, I could see that the flatness did not come just from my losing the opportunity for loving service. Facing myself with distaste, I realized that much of my sense of loss stemmed from traits I preferred to sweep under the rug. I liked seeing myself as rather saintly. I enjoyed believing that my satisfactions were in keeping with spiritual principles. Now I had to face the truth: even the most hated drudgery had given me something easy and unconfusing to dislike! Far from being thwarted by unwelcome demands on my time, I had been stimulated by them! By noting how much I missed them now, I could see how much unrecognized satisfaction I had garnered from them.

Family frictions and conflicts also appeared in a new light. Demands that I become a sort of slave for other members of my household had sharpened my vision of who I was as a child of God. Having to fight for time to employ the gifts I was given had made me keenly aware that the gifts were meant for me to use. Now that those demands from other persons no longer challenged me, my sense of being called to creative work was growing rather weak!

I missed feeling outraged. Without it I could fight no invigorating battles against the cause of my indignation and could make no triumphant dashes for freedom from it. Minus these aggravations, I was deprived of hills and valleys, peaks and ravines in my daily life. I felt dully leveled off, like mile upon mile upon mile of flat country. The lethargy of a peaceful existence sapped my creative energies more than labors and irritations ever had. With embarassment I wondered if much of my old boundless energy had not come from the adrenalin helpfully poured into my bloodstream through a feeling that I was being put upon.

Other disturbing discoveries crowded in. I had

always made friends easily. I had imagined that if I were congenial with a person I could move into a deep relationship without going through a preliminary period of getting acquainted. It seemed to me that I had often done this. And I never understood talk about someone's being lonely in a new job, church, or community because he or she was surrounded by strangers. Even my bitter experiences in the civil rights struggle in the fifties had been unable to erase my puppy-like feelings that nobody was a stranger. If I saw any signs of rapport between myself and another person, I nimbly leapt at once to the conclusion that we could understand each other perfectly. I had looked forward to gathering round me a band of all-new friends in my new life.

But undertaking a few new relationships among many old ones, which was what I had always done in the past, is radically different from having only new acquaintances. In the latter case I was overwhelmed with uncertainties. There is no reliable way to interpret what lies behind the words and actions of a stranger. Was Sue, or Jim, or Meg really pleased with my personality? Or were they inclined to agree quickly simply because they cared more about pleasant conversation than about the issues involved? The difference between polite amiability and genuine affinity can hardly be overstressed.

The same uncertainty applied if someone seemed irritable. Was that just Tom's accustomed mode of response or did I rub him the wrong way? Back home I could have asked a mutual friend about Tom's typical behavior. Here there was no one from whom I could get that information. In vain I told myself, "Just assume it isn't personal unless there's more evidence that it is." I was not equal to following that good advice.

Slowly learning where a certain new acquaintance stood on matters of first importance to me had always been part of the adventure of meeting new people. I now found that this can only be true when one is supported by some secure relationships. Since everyone I knew here was an unsolved mystery, gatherings of people were not the exciting experiences of budding fellowship I had anticipated. They were an ordeal!

Even between persons who happen to be quite like-minded, a new relationship wanders about in a maze of uncertainties. And as I skidded this way and that in the many possible interpretations of each unfamiliar personality, I found myself longing with growing desperation for at least one settled, dependable relationship that I could rest in while I laboriously explored all the others. There had been times in my life when I felt the presence of God sufficiently for him to be the person I could rest in. But as St. John pointed out in 1 John 4:20, when we can't relate to our fellow human beings, we can expect difficulty relating to God. Just as I felt alone in the midst of people now, I also felt alone in the midst of God. Even a person I didn't like particularly would do, I realized, if only I could move with him or her confidently in familiar grooves.

Familiar! Wasn't that word the key to most of the emptiness and lostness I felt? My new life held hardly anything familiar. I had moved from a house to an apartment, from a town near the mountains to the edge of a great city, from living in a family to living alone, from a setting where I had long known most of the people I dealt with to one where all my contacts were new, from a prescribed life where I had few choices to one where I had bewildering freedom.

I paused in my review, vaguely sensing that there were unrecognized changes in my life—changes even greater than those I had just named.

4

A Different Drummer

An important step in self-understanding came when I grasped the fact that as bad as humdrum routines can be, far worse is the terrible monotony of unending newness. Change, change, change had become for me the most deadly of all repetitions. Everywhere I met new sights, new sounds, new customs, new plans, new habits, new people. New, new, new, new, new. It was like dripping water or a ticking clock. Sometimes it was almost like the noise of pile driving or steel riveting. I wanted to stuff cotton in my ears to escape the bong, bong, bong of newness.

Insights and memories pushed up from deep inside me. How great was my need and my longing for familiar things! Without them life resembled a huge jigsaw puzzle tossed in the air and fallen in a jumbled mess without pattern or continuity. That was how my life looked to me.

I was born in 1906. Those were the horse and buggy days, the days of rural and small-town life, of close-knit families, impassioned patriotism, strict ethical codes, respect for elders, and stress on courtesy. They were the days of belief in discipline, self-control, hard work, frugality, chastity, self-sacrifice, and noble mottoes. My thoughts and feelings were molded in that culture. Built into me were assumptions, expectations and hopes seldom confirmed in today's society. My new home was within one hundred miles of my childhood home. Yet almost nothing in my present physical or psychological environment resembled what I had learned to take for granted.

Nearly everything in the common daily experience of an ordinary American had drastically changed in the last sixty years. The extent of such changes often escapes us until some painful experience confronts us. A joke that went the rounds when I was young suggests just how radical some of the changes are. The joke described an anxious mother urging her aviator son to be careful when flying. "Always remember, darling," the punch-line went, "to fly low and slow."

I sympathize with that poor mother. Safety guidelines that for centuries had proved practical and wise, suddenly, with the coming of air travel, became not merely modified but reversed. That kind of change twists the wisdom of yesterday into the idiocy of today and disintegrates any hope of coping with our problems. It is the kind of change that old people, with excellent reason, tend to reject.

Equally radical changes have occurred in other areas of our lives. Take everyday economics. When I was a child I never heard a challenge to homely advice for economic security: "Be thrifty; save your money; don't get in debt." It was self-evident wisdom. But when inflation rates exceed interest rates, we lose money by saving it. And incurring debts can be economical because the money is worth more when we borrow it than it will be when it's time to pay it back.

The kind of change (appropriately called progress) that merely adds to what we have already learned is easy to adjust to. But the heavy impact of the kind of change that contradicts what we have previously learned can be seriously destructive. It undermines our sense of security and our confidence in our own judgment. Laboratory experiments have shown that even rats have emotional breakdowns and become disoriented if they have learned to expect a certain result in certain circumstances and then are repeatedly given the opposite result.

When I was small, people learned to expect certain results from their common daily activities that are not forthcoming from those activities today. Take shopping. In the early years of this century, shopping was similar to the type of therapy where the primary aim is to give the suffering patient a sense of being totally accepted. The slogan, "The customer is always right," was taken seriously, and sales people who didn't subscribe to it were promptly fired. In most stores customers got immediate attention, solicitous service, and the over-all feeling that others were concerned about their needs and preferences. They could enter a store feeling dejected, and after half an hour or so of being treated like a king or queen, leave with a vastly improved self-image.

Today, over-busy clerks are likely to exude the message that customers are always wrong and a bother, too. Shoppers feel discounted and snubbed and may leave asking inwardly, "What's the matter with me that I'm treated that way?"

It has not been many years since people could take

their telephone receiver off the hook and hear a human voice say, "What number, please?" And when they gave it, the voice replied, "Thank you!" Not traffic lights but living, breathing policemen used to be at busy intersections. People got directions from them and maybe a friendly look and a smile. Not a button but living persons ran the elevators. They asked people what floor they wanted and took them there. A milk man and an ice man delivered, said, "Good morning!" and exchanged a few words with their customers. There was a shoe-shine boy (not a kit), a news boy (not a slot). And for too much housework, people didn't buy an appliance. They hired someone to help.

Conversation with all these people was possible because the pace was slower then, the pressure less, and everyone expected to enjoy bits of fellowship throughout the work day. If customers took shoes or a gadget to be repaired, there was unhurried consultation over the problem and what could be done about it. Repair men were heard to say that they chose their work because they liked people and enjoyed helping them. Today, the few who still do repairs in our throw-away society seem always to be hurried, impersonal, and tense.

Two or three generations ago, human contact was waiting everywhere. In the country and in small towns, where most of the population lived then, people spoke to each other as they passed or waited side-by-side. It didn't matter that they had never seen each other before. They were together, and that was reason enough to talk. Even in big cities, since services were performed by people rather than by machines, human exchange was inescapable.

True, those constant exchanges were often quite

brief and trivial if looked at separately. But taken together they formed a kind of fabric of fellowship that was like a friendly tapestry covering and warming the walls of people's lives. The over-all message was that persons were surrounded by other persons who liked and respected them and wanted their needs met.

This message may have been only a by-product of the courtesy that was expected from public servants of all kinds in those days. Perhaps it was no more sincere than it would be today. I'm not saying that the world was better then. It was better in some ways, worse in others. But the message was there all the same. And true or false, when it was believed, it contributed richly to a person's sense of belonging and of self-worth. The reiterated message widely heard today has the opposite effect. Even in their doctor's office many people feel that they are just another card in a computer.

Pondering these facts, I suddenly perceived the even more disturbing changes that heretofore I had only vaguely sensed. They were changes in the over-all culture of my country since I was a child. Alteration in American premises, goals, and values today reflected themselves in every area of life, even in the smallest instance of human contact. Officials and workers of all kinds now revealed an almost total lack of something I had been taught to take for granted—the desire to please. Gone were the little amenities that once had made these tiny human contacts pleasant, heart-warming experiences. I felt nostalgia not for a place but for a time in history, a lost way of life that once, not many years ago, had been virile, full-bodied and sweet.

When I was forming my understanding of truth

and untruth, right and wrong, the message reiterated by Americans on all sides was that there are rewards for simple goodness, justice, kindness, unselfishness, and what was then unapologetically called "clean living." The importance of maintaining an upright, self-sacrificing life—hard-working, simple, and other-worldly was proclaimed not only from pulpits and platforms but also was implied in fiction, nonfiction, and drama, even in advertisements.

Then, as always, there were skeptics, cynics, and radical intellectuals who rebelled against these values. But that only served to accent the fact that indeed the values were established. Everyone either believed in them, or gave them lip service, or else conspicuously revolted against them. But in the world I now saw around me, it was as if these values didn't exist.

I drove down great, gray highways that growled and vibrated across once green land. I visited supermarkets laden with extravagantly packaged, overpriced luxuries. My eye was assaulted by slogans and advertisements implying that there is no life apart from the five senses, that the best things in life are sensual, and that you might as well be dead if you don't have youth plus status plus luxury plus gratification of your desires. If I went to a movie I got the same message couched in language that would not have been used in the presence of a woman when I was young. If I opened a magazine, the same.

Conspicuously missing were an assortment of premises and assumptions upon which my life had always rested. Some were quite ordinary, such as that honesty is the best policy. Others were loftier: that discerning persons recognize principles and qualities more important than success, happiness or life itself.

I had been reared to believe that at the core of life God placed principles that always have been and always will be true, unvarying, dependable for all people everywhere. I was taught that the very structure of the universe contains these principles, and that failure to recognize and live by them puts us out-of-step with our Maker, our true selves, our fellow human beings, and even the very fabric of creation.

I was the product of a culture that had a solid feel to it. People knew, at least in a general way, what was expected of them in whatever roles they found themselves. The laws and guidelines for acceptability and approval were more clearly posted, more often discussed and more carefully adhered to by most people then than is true today. And there was much less uncertainty about how one should behave to ensure one's self-respect and the respect of others. Nearly all my moral assumptions, my expectations for my country, my interpretations of the behavior of others, and the conclusions I drew about life in general felt curiously dislocated from the culture I now discerned around me. No wonder I felt uneasy and out of focus. I was lonely for a way of looking at life that seemed to have vanished suddenly.

I know now that there was nothing sudden about its disappearance. For a long time erosion had been going on. What was sudden was my having leisure enough to notice what had happened. For fifteen years before I came here, all my time and thought had been divided between the various crises in my family and the civil rights crisis on my doorstep. I had scarcely glanced outside my immediate tasks and problems. And during those years open acceptance of changes in values, standards, and behavior had begun, which previously had been developing, more covertly, for decades.

Until the technology explosion of the twentieth century ushered in a new era, a person could grow old in much the same world he grew up in. But I was engulfed in a culture as different from the one I knew in my childhood as if I had moved to some oriental land. Manners, customs, appearances, occupations, attitudes, values, and morals were all remote from the ones I was taught to take for granted. Even the language was virtually a dialect of the one I had learned earlier. For all practical purposes I was now an unassimilated alien in a strange land. When I looked squarely at that truth, a wave of homesickness swept through me like nausea.

"The Shade of a Great Rock"

In making plans for a new life, I had assumed that I would build it around some church. Now that my biological family was dispersed, I turned to the church for fellowship and a sense of belonging as naturally as a traveler returns to his native land.

Earlier, I had thought the terms "church home" and "church family" rather sentimental. Now I saw them as straightforward expressions of solid truth. I needed a church home and a church family to structure the huge, empty places in my life. I needed people who shared my over-all goals and value system; I needed help in maintaining a sense of continuity with my early roots; above all, I needed a church to guide and stimulate my search for a deeper, more committed inner life.

An important factor in my decision to move to the Washington area was a famous ecumenical community called The Church of The Saviour. I had read of and visited this community and was impressed by the richness and variety of their activities and services. The church incorporated the best features of many denominations, and gatherings were fresh, unpredictable, and vibrant, as though newly come from the hand of God. They seemed just the kind of church I had long wanted to find.

But after worshiping and working with them for more than two years, I realized I could not bring myself to sever denominational connections and join them. I learned with a shock how strong my ties were with my own denomination. Faced with the growing gulf between life as I had known it and life as it was now, I saw how much I needed one area of stability, one unaltered link with my past. I began to search for a church home that would comfort my heart as well as feed my spirit. After a month or two, I thought I had found it.

It was a beautiful little church with sparkling stained-glass windows, a fine organ and a breath-taking choir. And blowing through the church was an air of expectancy and cordiality that made me feel I could readily become a part of its fellowship. I settled into my pew and drank in the long familiar lovely words and symbols as a desert traveler might drink from a new-found spring.

I smiled quizzically at myself as I realized that for the first time I knew I needed church buildings, including stained glass, altars, rituals, and fellowship with people who needed them, too. The style of worship in my denomination is more liturgical than in most Protestant churches, and while I had always thought our liturgies beautiful, I was inclined toward the view that the lesser the form, the freer the spirit. Above all, I had stoutly believed it wrong to build costly churches as long as people anywhere were hungry and cold.

Now I was painfully reminded that there is more than one kind of human need. The church alone can offer shelter from a certain kind of bitter wind, and my deep hunger could be assuaged only by the strength and peace I found inside her walls. As secular culture rolled over me day after day—the ruthless competition, the constant urging of advertisements to gratify self-centered desires, the restless, tense faces, all rooted in dead-end philosophies—I longed achingly for confirmation of the Christian vision of what we ought to be and how we ought to live. I wanted to be where this vision was declared to all the senses, through a variety of ancient symbols that had deep, untroubled roots inside me. In the bewildering brokenness of my patterns of living, the church alone stood steady and unaltered, reaching back into my earliest childhood—a visible, touchable, long-remembered expression of my faith and a steadfast symbol of the unchanging love of God.

In searching for a church home, I learned how great my need was for all that the church represents. Sometimes the very sight of a church would make me feel less in exile. I would think, "In there people speak of the things I try to live by. They help each other believe in the Lord of all. And they try to love and serve and understand him more." And I would have a snug, warm, comforted feeling—as though I had looked into my living room and seen my family gathered round the fireplace talking and laughing together.

Joseph Lox was a gray-eyed young minister with irrepressible blond hair and a matching manner of eager energy. Standing at the door after the service, he took my hand and smiled contagiously straight into my eyes. Then with his other hand, he reached out in a gesture of unselfconscious ease and lifted an unusual cross I was wearing on a chain.

"I like this. Did it come from Texas? I know there's a man there who makes them."

"Yes. Gert Behanna gave it to me. Do you know her?"

"No, but I know who she is. Sometime tell me more about her."

His manner and tone implied that we were old friends. It was a small outreach, yet with the leverage of my need it lifted from me any small chill of strangeness that remained. I was filled with a lovely warmth and felt my roots stretch down to take hold in my new community. I turned from the door and went into the parish hall for the coffee hour that followed each service.

Joe introduced me to his tiny round-faced wife, Sue, whose graciousness was like a breeze across a ripe wheat field. She in turn presented me to others who stood sipping coffee and smiling as if they meant it. Everyone seemed to want me to have a sense of belonging. I was captured. This was my church home. My mind was made up.

Joe's and Sue's friendliness had special meaning for me. To their personal charm and their symbolic impact as minister and wife was added the fact that my biological family had a heavy sprinkling of clergymen. My father, grandfather, two uncles, and a cousin were clergymen, and one of my sons was debating the possibility of entering the ministry. I took it for granted that I had an inside track with people of the cloth. I even assumed that just as the church in general was my extended family, the clergy and their households were my immediate family. A few months later this assumption was to contribute much to my close brush with destruction.

I moved at once to increase my acquaintance with

Joe and Sue. We exchanged visits, and I made a point of supporting any church programs he seemed anxious to promote. I wanted to be a helpful addition to the parish. Also I wanted to help Joe and Sue as a friend and as a defender when the need arose. That it would arise I was sure. Joe admitted he was bent on renewing the parish. He was sure to meet opposition from those who preferred immobility to improvement.

By renewing, I assumed he meant deepening people's faith and inducing them to express it more fully in their lives. There are always those who consider such efforts meddling. As a person who had stout roots in our denomination and little difficulty defending the faith, I hoped I could be a useful friend.

A lovely feeling of being needed pervaded me. I could serve this little church as well as be served by them. There was mutuality in our relationship, and promise of the close-binding interplay of giving and receiving that is inseparable from true family life.

Both Joe's leadership in discussion groups and his sermons were curiously exciting. He spoke with energy and conviction. Yet there were subtle overtones that were mind-stretching. I sensed that he implied something vast in addition to what he actually said. I could never grasp what the mysterious implication was, although it seemed to dovetail with the air of impending events that hung over the little church. Reaching for the implication kept me on tiptoe and I liked the feeling. For many months I imagined that I could not grasp it merely because I was new to the church.

Among many pleasant feelings of adventure, I also experienced vague uneasiness. It was just out of reach. What caused it was as vaporous as the feeling itself. Sudden silences were one cause. I have no fear or suspicion of silences as such. But these fell at surprising times. Joe would mention a hope or plan he had for the church. I would make an eager response, meant to build on his thought. Then the silence would fall. His face would take on a blank look or a sudden look of speculation. I would have a tiny shock of disappointment. We had failed to meet each other, and I didn't know why.

Sometimes the lack of connection between Joe and me came from my side. Early one morning, following our six o'clock Wednesday Communion service, the usual handful of us were having a simple breakfast of buns and coffee in the parish hall. This was an understandably poorly attended service for the faithful few who wanted midweek Communion before going to work. The same five or six persons came regularly, and we had reached the place where we all, including Joe, spoke of intimate concerns we would not have discussed elsewhere.

On this particular morning the subject of concern was a man whose only daughter had, according to her physicians, a rare and incurable genetic disease. The longest life on record for a child with the disease was not much beyond the girl's age. When Joe spoke sadly of his own inability to get through to Herbert, the father, one of the young women at our table, Ruth, asked:

"You mean you can't get him to hope?"

"I mean I can't get him to give up false hopes. He just tunes me out when I try to make him face the truth."

"What is the truth, Joe?"

"That he's not going to have that kid around much

longer. He's even made a will leaving everything to Jenny. If he doesn't give himself some kind of preparation, when she dies, he's going to collapse—and it won't be long now."

"How do you know he isn't right?" I felt impelled to ask. "Doctors don't know everything—don't even claim to. And if the disease is all that rare, there's no way of knowing what to expect in every case. Herbert may be killed driving home today, and Jenny may outlive us all. Why should he face grief he may never meet?"

"You could be right," Joe said in the kind of flat voice one uses in reciting the alphabet.

The obvious fact that he had tuned out my protest troubled me less than the fact that I knew I had been ashamed to make the protest I really meant. I decided to back up and try again.

"I guess what I'm really trying to say is that one definition of a church is 'a praying community.' I know Herb prays constantly for Jenny. Just now you sounded almost as if there were something psychotic about his assuming his prayers might be answered. I think he's behaving as we all should be doing."

There was a long pause, then Ruth said, "I think I agree."

There was another pause and Joe said, "Of course I believe in prayer. You know I do. What worries me is Herb's unwillingness to face change in general. Jenny's illness is just one example. And there's a lot of other people in the church just as bad as Herb, but they're a lot older. They want everything to stay just the same. I think they're half-dead inside and want the church to match! *Any* little change in the worship service, and Herb hits the ceiling—says it doesn't seem like his church any more. I expect that sort of thing from Mrs. Hutchenson and Miss Angela Fenn and Professor McCorkin. But Herb's only thirty-two. He shouldn't be standing with the old guard. He should get excited about the new. When people can't face change, it's because they're atrophied, and atrophication isn't healthy. I think Herb needs psychiatric help."

"I don't see anything abnormal about wanting things he loves to stay the way he loves them," I pointed out.

"I don't believe Herb has any great love for the church. He's just stuck with the idea that things ought to continue the way they've always been."

Ruth's husband, Ed, objected. "Joe, I think Herb does love the church. I remember hearing him say he feels like a new man after church most Sundays. Sometimes I do, too."

Charlie Rutherford, the other man present, shook his head. "Most church services put me to sleep. That one you had Thanksgiving sure didn't, though. Gee, that was great! I like rock music anyway."

"That's what I mean," Joe said. "That was a deeply meaningful service—in step with the times—but a lot of people didn't like it. One woman said it spoiled Thanksgiving for her. Herb left before it was over. Said it gave him a headache. I still think he needs psychiatric help."

"Some of my best friends are psychiatrists," I said lightly. "I lived next door to one for years. He said we all need help—everybody. Doesn't the church proclaim the same bad news along with the good news that help is at hand?"

Joe gave his soft, pleasant laugh. "It surely does. I know I need help—of all kinds, God help me! Anybody besides God want to give me a hand?"

Ruth and I agreed to act as stand-ins for the Lord until a miracle could be pushed through to take some of Joe's work load. So the breakfast broke up on a note of levity. The others went smiling off to work while Joe, Ruth, and I cheerfully pitched in where we were.

But as I worked I was faintly conscious of a corner of myself that wasn't smiling. All four of the people Joe had named as unable to face change were persons whose lives, I had learned, little resembled what they had been only a few years ago. They couldn't face change? Nothing in their lives was unchanged! Maybe they needed one anchor somewhere.

I didn't know how to explain the problem to Joe. I didn't yet understand it myself. All I knew was that though it was my own nature to delight in innovations and experiments, I had suddenly reached the saturation point. I was like a person who had eaten too much of a favorite food. One more mouthful and I would be ill. Maybe the people Joe mentioned felt the same way. They had good reason to. But Joe seemed unable to see their need.

This was five years before Drs. Thomas Holmes and Richard Rahe published their now famous stress scale. The scale indicates that large amounts of stress are involved in adjusting to all changes, even happy ones like vacations and increase of pay. These psychiatrists warn that too many changes, good or bad, in too short a time, create grave danger of emotional illness. If that scale had existed then, it would have helped me to understand myself and Joe to understand his church.

I was also troubled by the timbre of Joe's voice when he spoke of Herb and members of the old guard. Besides frustration, it held impatience, and something more. Contempt? And did he link obstructionism with age? He sounded as though he did. But when I asked him, he vigorously denied it. Then—a little hesitantly—he used me as evidence.

"I'm counting on you to help make changes," he said.

On the surface, I accepted his denial and treasured the feeling of belonging that I got from him. But looking back, I think his answer increased my uneasiness on a less conscious level. I suspected he was jumping to unjustified conclusions. Knowing I had opposed the old guard on civil rights in the 1950s, he thought I would oppose it in this case, too. His sudden silences, I now know, resulted from doubt that he was right.

But Joe and I sometimes had wonderful rapport and a lot of fun together. He conned me into undertaking a variety of jobs, large and small, and I enjoyed them all—both because I loved Joe and because I needed to be useful. Often he implied that he regarded me as one of the important keys to the success of his renewal plans. He would talk enthusiastically about some project, then would turn to me with a teenage grin and say, "If you imagine I'm insinuating you should take the lead in getting this off the ground, you're totally—right!" Or he would pause on the way to his office and say, "Am I glad to see you! I was feeling down. Now I'm up!"

These uninvited small tributes heartened me. I was helpful. I was an insider. To this little church family I truly belonged.

Mistaken Identity

I have long held that a phony compliment is really an insult. It implies that we are vain, that we are stupid enough to believe anything, and that the person giving it can think of nothing good to say sincerely. Above all, it makes us—or at least it makes me feel like an outsider. When I get a phony compliment I have the same lonely, excluded feeling I have when I learn of a criticism someone has made behind my back.

I had always prided myself on seldom being the target of deliberate flattery. I had—so I thought—the kind of personality that discourages it. Even people for whom flattery is a way of life seldom practiced it on me. Therefore it was especially disconcerting to find that in the midst of my church family, I often found myself being buttered thickly on both sides.

It was obvious that the butterers were trying to be kind, trying to make me feel appreciated and at home. So I strove to be pleased by their well-intentioned attempts. But I couldn't help wishing they would just be natural. The very fact that they made all that effort somehow implied they didn't regard me as one of themselves. And more than anything else I wanted to be one of them.

"My but you're strong!" a husky, six-foot young man exlaimed as I hurried up a short flight of steps to the parish hall carrying an ordinary shopping bag full of donations for the church bazaar. "I couldn't run up steps that way with a heavy load."

"Why you poor, little thing!" I countered.

"No, I mean it," he insisted. "You're the strongest woman I know. I've heard other people say so, too."

What he said was plainly unbelievable. I had moved at no more than average speed for any healthy person, and every housekeeper daily hauls bags of groceries weighing more than my heavy load. I had a feeling of being patted on the head for accomplishing something that Daddy, Mama, and Aunt Minnie did routinely. Being strong isn't quite the sort of thing you praise healthy adults for, anyway. You just assume they are fairly strong and don't think about it. But of course he meant well.

On another occasion a small knot of women gathered round me and exclaimed over my dress. Now, there was absolutely nothing remarkable about that dress—except that I had bought it at a half-price sale, a fact the women didn't know. Yet on and on they went about it.

"Patty is the best dresser at St. Luke's, and that's a fact."

"She certainly is! She always looks just stunning." And so on and on.

This, too, was obviously kindly meant but patently false. Well knowing that it takes time, thought, and money to be a stunning dresser, and preferring to use what little I have of these elements on other endeavors, I have never even tried to be a stunning dresser. And I much doubt if that is something one can achieve without trying.

But I was eager to love and be loved by my church family, and I quickly turned my mind from anything unpleasing that happened in my church home. I wanted to feel grateful that I belonged there and in being there was blessed.

Assurances that I was an insider in my church were important, because I wasn't feeling comfortable with people in general. In a typical day, the people I met casually often responded to me in ways that were vaguely inappropriate, almost as if they weren't talking to me at all but to some quite different personality. I had noticed the phenomenon when I first came to my new home. But now, after a year, it was getting much worse. The experience was ghostly and hard to define, yet unquestionably real. It was like the feeling we have in a dense fog when some bulky object is only half seen. It is glimpsed, lost, glimpsed again.

A supermarket check-out girl finished ringing up my groceries. Without looking at me, she said in a routine way, "Anything else? Cigarettes?" Here she glanced up. At once her manner changed. "Oh, no-o-o!" she cooed. "Of course you don't want those nasty old things!"

Now, in point of fact, I don't smoke. But why should anyone reach that conclusion at first sight? Besides, why the dreadful, condescending coo? I looked to see if there were a small child behind me she could be addressing. There wasn't.

Waiting in a long line to cash a check, I noted the bank teller's swift deftness as he counted money in the denominations each person asked for.

"All in tens, please," I told him when my turn came.

He reached for the tens, then as his eyes fell on me, for the first time he dropped his rhythmic efficiency. He paused, smiled and asked gently, "Are you sure you don't want some fives and ones?" He was clearly expressing solicitude, but why did he single me out for it?

At a junior college theater, where I went on invitation from a member of the class, a girl in her late teens gave me a startled look when I sat beside her. Glancing at me several times in a troubled way, she finally blurted out, "I must warn you. This is an adult show."

I wanted to laugh but her earnestness told me she meant no joke. "I'm an adult," I pointed out. "I've seen adult shows."

She looked relieved. "Oh. Then that's all right."

The show was *Under Milkwood* by Dylan Thomas, and by today's standards hardly a shocker. The girl's behavior made me feel unwelcome. Could it be that for some reason they wanted only students at their shows? But I came on invitation. And besides, the poster plainly said "The Public is Invited." Did I look more prudish than the rest of the public?

Then there were the two incidents in the Post Office. One day after stamping my several letters I handed them in at the window. The man who gathered them up saw I had failed to seal one. Instead of simply handing it back he took time out, with people standing in line behind me, to explain slowly, gently, why letters should be sealed.

"Now you must always seal your letters. Try to remember that. If you don't, the contents may fall out and get lost. Then it might not be delivered and you'd worry about not getting an answer. We wouldn't want that to happen to you."

Not long after that, I had a different kind of experience with another mail clerk. When I asked for a sheet of a hundred stamps, he didn't reach for them and state the cost as he had done with other people. He looked at me closely and said:

"Stamps are expensive now, you know. Do you have the money?"

"Why on earth do you think I mightn't?" I asked sharply.

He didn't answer. Nor did he reach for the stamps. I opened my purse and took out a $20 bill. Instantly he plucked the stamps from the drawer and handed them to me. I was so outraged I nearly reported him. I did not understand his behavior, but I knew it was insulting. He had singled me out and as good as said I looked like the kind of person who would try to buy what I couldn't pay for.

Did I just imagine I was being treated in a new way? Any of these happenings, taken alone, could be dismissed as merely odd behavior. And odd behavior in others is the spice of life. Why not just smile, shrug, and write it all off as coincidence?

I tried and could not. The incidents were too frequent. Believing they all resulted from aberrations in other people would put me in the everybody's-out-of-step-but-Johnnie school of thought. Moreover, these kinds of responses were too new in my experience. If they were in the normal course of human relations, why hadn't they happened all along? Finally, while various causal explanations could be applied to each incident separately, when taken together they had an unanimous message. I couldn't quite put my finger on what it was. I wasn't sure I wanted to. But there was something vaguely denigrating about it. I got a terrible, lonely feeling whenever I tried to figure it out.

The puzzle was rather intriguing at times, I told myself. So many different kinds of experience had that strange, new flavor. For example, all my life I had been prone to make incredible boners. In addition, I had always been physically clumsy and precipitant and sometimes left behind me a trail of minor disasters that could be followed. My grandmother used to warn, "Slow down, little girl! More haste, less speed, you know."

But I had early learned to redeem both those weaknesses by telling funny stories about them. Whenever conversation lagged, I would start the fascinating game of "Did you ever do or say anything as bad as this?" Then I would review my most recent disaster. People would laugh and rejoin, "Wait! I can top you!" or "Thank goodness somebody else does that sort of thing! I thought I was the only one."

But now the response was almost always different. People only looked uncomfortable and assumed I was apologizing for a problem. "Don't you worry about it, dear; anybody can do such things," was a typical reply. It was as though there was something wrong with me and I needed reassurance. It made my stories no fun for anybody. I felt cut off from my favorite conversation pieces.

Once, even as I laughingly told a new friend that I had dropped everything I picked up that day, her look of deep concern really scared me. "Oh, I'm sure it's nothing, honey. Just forget it. You're OK."

Briefly I wondered if dropping things were a symptom of some illness this woman recognized. Maybe I had a disease others were aware of, although I was not. That would explain the over-solicitude of some people toward me and also the check-out girl's strange behavior about the cigarettes. And it would explain something that recently happened in a Bible study group.

Arriving unavoidably late to the informal class, I dropped unobtrusively to the floor, where two-thirds of the students were already seated. Instantly, little exclamations of alarm rippled through the room. A spotlight of consternation and advice blazed on me. I was urged to accept chairs, was offered cushions, was informed that I could not possibly be comfortable on the floor. In vain I assured people that I was a floor sitter by nature, that I had seen empty chairs I could have used. It was all quite embarrassing and annoying. The thread of the discussion in progress when I arrived was permanently lost. What on earth was the matter with these people—or with me?—that my simple act disrupted the class? True, I wasn't a kid any more, but other middle-aged people were sitting on the floor, so age alone could not explain it.

Nor was that the end of it. Throughout the evening, if I shifted position half an inch, a chain reaction of inquiries and suggestions ensued: "Are you sure you're OK there?" "Here, take this pillow." And when the class was over, again commotion! Half the hands in the room reached out to help me up. Now, I may be awkward, but I'm also flexible and rising from the floor has never been a problem for me. But again there was an outcry: "Will you please look at Patty! She doesn't need our help!"—as though I were a baby taking my first tottering step!

I was baffled. It just didn't make sense. That is, it didn't unless indeed I had some serious illness that others knew about. But I felt too good for that. And my doctor had given me a sweeping OK on my annual check-up. So I put the disease theory from my mind and refused to reinstate it, even though evidence for it continued to appear.

One day I delivered to Goodwill Industries a box of miscellany I had collected. Though not heavy, the box was large and difficult to edge through my VW's small door without damage to the paint. Parked on a side street, I gently shifted the box this way and that, seeking just the right angle. A young woman suddenly stepped up and offered brightly, "Can I help?"

Trying not to lose my grip on the box, I twisted my head toward her. With genuine appreciation I said, "How nice of you! But, no thank you. This is a one-person job. The box is very light."

I returned to my task and was just beginning to make headway when I felt the woman close to my elbow. "Now, now, you must let me help! You might strain yourself."

"No, thank you," I repeated less gratefully. "I can manage better alone. I understand the problem."

"You'll hurt yourself!" she insisted.

"No," I replied. "I just can't use any help—and I don't need any."

A telephone pole would not have ignored my assurances more completely. From the corner of my eye I could see her still standing there, anxiously clutching her hands against her breast, while she whispered, half to herself, "Oh! o-o-o, oo!—do, do be careful!"

In spite of her, I miraculously got the box through the door without scratching paint. In silent triumph I carried it inside the building to the donation center. When I came out, the woman was gone. But I continued to be upset. Somehow the experience implied more than met the eye. I sensed overtones and implications that were symbolic of something. And, again, a hidden message reverberated insistently.

I was haunted by the feeling that my humanness had been bypassed. This woman had refused to accept my decision that assistance would not help. Essential to human dignity is the right to think and act for oneself. One can't exist as a whole person unless the right to make decisions concerning one's own welfare is recognized and respected. A challenge to this right is the grossest insult to personhood. Nothing else is so dehumanizing.

The passion of conviction that seized me as those thoughts pressed into my mind astonished me. If only the woman had moved on when I first declined her offer! Then her gesture would have left good feelings in us both. The message would have been that she cared enough to help and respected me enough to accept my refusal. We both would have known that on the vast ocean of humanity we had met, smiled warmly, and saluted.

More than any previous incident, this one quickened my feeling of being slowly forced out of something very precious to me. I felt lonely and demeaned. My mind clung to episodes that had some of the same quality as this one. My thoughts went round and round in them, trying to understand why they happened. Yet I knew I didn't really want to understand. What I wanted was to convince myself that they weren't symbols, weren't prophesies, weren't messages, weren't significant.

I found myself linking them with the problems of minorities. I had often heard Southern blacks and people with severe physical handicaps complain of various forms of special treatment. I used to wonder why they objected, even when it was clear that it was kindly meant. Now I knew. It undermined their sense of commonality with other persons. It made them feel isolated, demoted from the rest of the human race. But why was I getting this treatment? I wasn't a member of any minority. I was a vigorous, middle-class, middle-aged white woman, about as unhandicapped as anyone could be.

And why did people keep trying to take care of me? I wasn't the type. On the contrary, I was so visibly strong-bodied, strong-minded, and independent that all my life people had spotted me as one who would take care of them. I had always been looked to for many kinds of help—emotional, physical, moral, material. I liked the role of rescuer and felt at home in it. Why was I being treated now as though I were some kind of victim?

The only sort of victim I could see myself being was a victim of mistaken identity. I often felt now as though I were the physical double of someone totally unlike me in character and temperament—some helpless, dependent, inadequate creature. It gave me eerie, dislocated feelings. The total lack of connection between myself as I really was and the way people often responded to me was one of the aspects of my experiences that I found most baffling.

One day I was visiting a friend in what was currently referred to as a "retirement community," where the average age of the residents was over eighty. As I stood waiting for the elevator to take me to my friend's floor, a woman in her forties joined me. She totally ignored my presence, and without even glancing at me, pressed the button again as though no one else were there. When the elevator came, still without looking at my face, she put her hands on my shoulders, as one might with a two-year-old, and propelled me into it.

Taken aback, I cried, "What are you doing?"

In the special low, slow voice some people use with very ill persons and very small children she replied, "Now, I just helped you on the elevator. There you are! Now you're all right!"

I wanted to grasp her shoulders, propel her into a corner and say in that same low, slow tone that I was all right before her action but not any more. I was mad enough to throw a cup. But I contented myself with only a glare—which was wasted on her, because not once did she glance at my face. It may be the most flagrant case of discounting a human being that I have ever seen. I ached with the realization that that was the way old people are treated in our society. In a couple of decades, I would be old. Was that the kind of indignity I had to look forward to?

I am astonished now that the circumstances of that experience, especially coming after many others, didn't force me to make the connection I was striving not to make. It did, however, push the truth a bit closer to conscious recognition. I admitted to myself that my mistaken identity experiences weren't intriguing at all: they made hideous feelings churn inside me. And I almost admitted that some of those feelings were fear.

The most unnerving example of my being made to feel that I was some kind of changeling occurred in my own apartment building. In the hall I was confronted by a small child, whose ownership of a puppy had just been discovered by the management. Pets were forbidden, and she was forced to give it up.

As I approached, she looked up with angry, tear-filled eyes.

"Why did you tell on my little dog? He didn't have any fleas, and he didn't make any noise."

The accusation rocked me. All I could say was, "Me?"

"Why don't you like animals?"

"But I love animals," I cried, "especially your little dog. I wouldn't have told on him for the world!"

Sissie returned my gaze with a small child's uninhibited disbelief. "It was mean of you," she said and walked away.

I was sick with pain. The accusation couldn't have been less deserved. Throughout my life I had kept pets. I had raised dozens of animals—puppies, kittens, hamsters, even wild rabbits, squirrels, and opossums. Whenever I had found a wounded or lost baby animal, I had routinely raised it until it could take care of itself, then turned it loose. With half a dozen families living in our section, why was I, of all people, chosen for such convinced suspicions? I had petted and played with Sissie's puppy and had told her often how cute he was.

Some adult must have put the notion in her head. But that explained little. Why had the adult singled me out? The image of myself as an animal hater who would ruthlessly break the heart of a child was the most out-of-character and most distressing of all my experiences of mistaken identity.

A Segregated Minority

By the time I was five I had learned that I could amuse people by pretending to speak from a pinnacle of years. In the words and tones of my grandmother, I would introduce my two cents worth into adult conversation with such comments as "I used to think that, too, but in my old age I'm not so sure."

Listeners would laugh and hug me. So I kept on doing it. I did it through my teens, twenties, thirties, forties, and the first nine-tenths of my fifties, always collecting smiles and sometimes chuckles in recognition of my small jest.

Then one day, soon after my experience at the elevator in the retirement home, I was talking with an acquaintance who made a remark I sharply disagreed with. Thinking a little lightness might reduce the tension, I grinned and replied, "I used to think that, too, but now in my old age. . . ."

Instead of reaching out with the eye twinkle I expected, the woman reached out with her hand. Patting me reassuringly on the shoulder, she crooned, "Now, you mustn't say that. You're not old."

So that was how I learned that I was old.

That phony reassurance got through my defenses where all my other experiences had failed. Now I saw the reason for my new feelings of loneliness, inadequacy, and helplessness. Now I saw the reason for my sense of being separated from the rest of mankind. I was being elbowed out of the human race.

Not that anyone intended to do it. But people no longer saw me as me, a person like themselves. They saw me as an old woman, a stereotype composed of all the misconceptions and surrounded by the many conflicting feelings that the old-woman image inspires in our day.

I was being related to as that image, that object, rather than as an individual person. Therefore I was outside the realm of human relationships!

My discovery was numbing. All along, of course, I had known I was growing older. But that is radically different from being old. Growing old is a lifetime matter—the younger one is, the more painful. When I was in my teens I would peer fearfully into my handmirror, searching for the first lines and gray hairs. I agonized over microscopic laugh lines around my eyes. (What man could love me with my face all marked up with wrinkles?) By the time I reached my fifties, however, I was used to growing old and thought no more about it. But now I had to deal with something in another category. I was old already, old right now!

How could that be? I didn't feel old. I had none of the aches or ailments that old people are supposed to have. All my faculties were still normal. My energy and interest were high. My whole being focused forward on what I intended to do, rather than backward on what I had done. And I had more friends who were under fifty than over fifty. So how could I be old? Everything indicated that I was middle-aged.

Yet with dull thuds the awareness pounded me that if I weren't actually old, at least that must be how I was perceived. It would explain too much not to be true. With that explanation everything fell into place. What I had been experiencing was the beginnings of segregation, or creeping apartheid! I had been feeling the pain of being pushed from midstream to the sidewaters of human contact and consciousness.

During the 1950s and 1960s, in my years of active involvement in the black southerner's struggle for recognition, I learned much that helped me now to grasp my situation. I could see that, like blacks, the old are thought of as one undifferentiated entity—*oldpeople,* spelled as one word. We are set apart in other minds, just as blacks are, and then are thought of as "they." When that happens to human beings, then fixed images, or stereotypes, cling to them like tar and feathers.

A classic example of stereotyping was the view of black people held by the majority of white people in the first half of this century. It pictured blacks (or Negroes, as they were then usually called) as lazy, funny, primitive, and mentally and morally inferior. Most whites held this stereotype with no feelings of guilt or sense of prejudice. To them the truth of their view seemed factual and self-evident. Black people in tragic numbers were brainwashed by the consensus into accepting that picture of themselves. As a result, their self-image was so poor and they expected so little of themselves that a vicious circle was set up from which escape was hard.

Something similar was happening now to the old. I had begun to feel shadowy and unreal. The group image had engulfed my personal characteristics. I was seen as having whatever traits each beholder attributed to *oldpeople*. That image was then addressed instead of me. (No wonder I kept looking behind me to see who the person was talking to!) As the experiences continued, I would have had to be superhuman not to see myself as I was seen. Then soon I would act out the picture of myself I saw. A hard and lonely battle for my human dignity was in store.

In the fifties, my black friends used often to make a protest that at first I found puzzling: "Why can't we be treated as individuals, not always as members of a group?"

Having never myself experienced being treated as anything but an individual person, I couldn't quite grasp what the distinction meant. But as I listened, I began to see what they referred to. One thing was the discounting of their individual characteristics and personhood—or the mistaken identity syndrome, though I didn't call it that then. The other was the absence of a you-and-I relationship. Southern whites, no matter how kind and fair they tried to be, tended to think in terms of "we," meaning whites, and "they," meaning blacks. That made black persons always one of them over there and white persons one of us over here. Blacks were never thought of as belonging to the we-group. I learned then that the two most terrible words in the language can be "they" and "them," for these are collective words from which we have withdrawn ourselves.

I learned too from blacks that characteristic of stereotypes are sweeping generalizations, as though all members of a group were alike. At times this is carried to incredible extremes.

A scholarly black English professor told me that once at a gathering, a white aquaintance seized him by the arm and guided him over to meet "someone you'll like." The someone turned out to be a black janitor who couldn't put two sentences together grammatically. After introducing them, the white man gravely said: "I'll buzz along now. I know you two will have a lot to talk about."

The professor said with a twinkle in his eye that the only thing he could think of to say to the janitor was, "You black, me black, we black."

I saw that already I had become the squirming victim of that kind of classifying. Any time I was told about "someone you'll like," it was safe to place a one hundred to one bet that the person was old and a ten to one bet that we had nothing else in common. It gave me the eerie feeling that my personality was totally blanked out.

Among the people I really wanted to know better in my church was an attractive woman in her mid-thirties. I liked her the minute I saw her. And I could tell by the sparkle in her expressive, intelligent eyes that she felt the same way about me. Repeatedly at the coffee hour that followed the service, she made a point of seeking me out. Our minds seemed to work alike, we had an identical sense of humor, and she seemed eager to know my thinking on a variety of subjects. She became an important part of my snug feeling that I was being whole-heartedly accepted into the family of my church. Not once did I have the smallest sense of mistaken identity in our conversations, and I took it for granted that we were headed for a permanent friendship. I was on the verge of hastening that happy time by inviting her to lunch when she telephoned to ask if she could stop by in about half an hour.

"There's something special I want to talk about," she said.

"Why, Al, how great that our two great minds are running in the same channel," I replied. "I've been dying to have a good, long talk with you. Come right along on over."

After we exchanged greetings and settled down with tea and cookies, Al said, "From the very first minute we met, I was sure you were the kind of person I've been hoping and praying for. And each time we talk, I'm surer."

Naturally I beamed. "I feel the same about you, Al. And I'm just flattered to death that you want to talk to me about something."

She seized the opening I purposely gave her. That was one of the things I liked about her. She wasn't one to dillydally.

"It's about my mother."

"Tell me, Al."

"Well, she moved here when I did. And she's rather shy. She doesn't know how to make friends the way you do. So I've been wondering if maybe you'd be friends with her. Then she wouldn't feel so alone and so—and so dependent on me. She says I'm all the friend she needs. But I just can't be that to her. Our worlds are miles apart. I need people my own age and so does she. You'd be just right for her. You're about the same age."

"Bring her to tea on Friday," I suggested, carefully focusing on my cup and trying not to sound the way I felt.

"Oh, thank you! I do thank you! You are the answer to my prayers."

But I wasn't as sure as Al that her solution was the Lord's handiwork. Her mother didn't sound like my favorite kind of person—even if we were the same age!

Al's cultivating me solely for her mother's sake cut deep. It made me feel less a full-scale human being, more blanked out as a personality, more just a segment in a segregated group. I had thought of Al spontaneously and joyfully as a friend. But to her I wasn't one of "us." I was one of "them."

This blanking out of the real me in favor of a category occurred in many ways. Some of them were quite small, but all were disturbing to me.

One day I was showing Hetty, a plump little woman of about forty, through my apartment. She planned to rent one like it, and I was explaining its advantages and disadvantages.

"The highway is too close and may disturb you," I pointed out. "The noise gets pretty bad at rush hours, but traffic noises never bother me unless I'm listening for something else I'd rather hear."

Hetty looked at me and smiled sagely. "My great uncle feels the same way. He says he's gotten so he likes commotion. Makes him feel more alive and part of things. I can't wait till I'm old enough not to mind noise. Already it doesn't disturb me like it used to."

On the face of it, Hetty's remarks were innocent, even amusing. But I didn't find them so. To me they were in the last straw department. They were another example of making me into a nonperson. Here I had casually mentioned an individual characteristic of mine, and my listener's mind at once clicked away at classifying it as an example of "how *oldpeople* feel about noise." In the twinkling of an eye, my idiosyncrasy was converted into a symptom. Moreover, her position was factually incorrect. Some old people grow more, not less, sensitive to noise; others remain the same. I had remained the same.

My exaggerated reaction to Hetty's trivial remarks showed me how sore to the touch I had become. I was keenly aware of the smallest acts, comments, looks, voice inflections, and choices of words that showed I was being tossed into a segregated minority. Far from becoming immune to these signs, I had become more vulnerable. The effect was cumulative—like continued pounding on the same bruised muscle. I winced more with each new blow, whether that blow was great or small. My back was to the wall. And what I defended was my personhood, my status as a child of God. I felt that my very self was being wrested from me.

In the entrance hall of a public building, I saw a huge poster. Evidently it was sponsored by some humanitarian organization bent on renewing hope of employment and also on fighting discrimination in jobs. In large letters it read:

"There is a Place For You. No matter where you come from or how life has dealt with you, this is *America,* and there is useful work you can do."

The illustration showed what was meant to be a cross section of humanity—persons who were short, tall, overweight, male, female, of many races and cultures; a man with a crutch, a woman in a wheel chair, a blind girl, two teenagers. But no one in the picture was old. Beneath it were the words, "Decent citizens will not tolerate job discrimination against anyone because of race, color, sex, religion, youth, or national origin."

An enormous wave of loneliness towered over me. Weren't old people Americans? And shouldn't decent citizens fight discrimination against them too? Were they outsiders to the point where their very existence was ignored? The fact that omitting them probably was unintentional, in a sense, only made it worse. It showed that, not just in outward expressions but also deep down in minds and hearts, old people were being bypassed. Bad as it was to be thought of and consciously excluded, it was worse to be not thought of at all.

Few of us can grasp experiences of others except through like experiences of our own. Only now could I perceive how starkly factual and unembellished were the black southerner's descriptions of the deadliness of being stereotyped and segregated. There are clear parallels between the experience of being black and the experience of being old in twentieth-century America, and I found myself looking at them closely.

The two minorities are about the same size, around 12 percent of the population. Just as blacks were long openly referred to as "the white man's burden," the old are now openly proclaimed the young person's burden. (That alone is enough to undercut our self-esteem and sabotage our joy in life.) The old share with blacks, women, and persons of certain other marked-down groups, the problem of high visibility. This means that we too are branded as inferior by preconceptions before we, as individuals, have a chance to demonstrate our skills and gifts. We are denied work regardless of our qualifications; we are segregated, treated like children, downgraded, discounted, condescended to.

But in addition to incorporating many of the evils

of other forms of discrimination, bigotry toward the aged has some features all its own. One is the degree of despair that prejudiced treatment engenders in the old. Unlike most other oppressed minorities, the old have not grown up with and partially adjusted to their low status. Therefore, many of them are not prepared for the humiliation of being discounted. The experience often comes, as it did to me, in a series of bruising shocks that rupture confidence, energy, and even the will to live. There are twice as many known suicides among the old as in the population as a whole. It is estimated that the figure actually is much higher than that, since unexpected death in an old person usually is assumed to be from natural causes and no investigation is deemed necessary.

Like racism and sexism, ageism saturates our culture. Once I knew that ageism was the explanation of my experiences, I also knew the terrible implications and prognosis of my situation. People hold fast to their prejudices and preconceptions. And to the old, discounting and rejection come as a progressive, terminal disease. That is another feature not shared by most other victims of discrimination.

Persons oppressed because of youth know with certainty that the problem will soon be outgrown. Persons oppressed because of poverty, ignorance, or cultural background know that at least the possibility exists, through hard work and study, to gain respect and change their situation. Persons oppressed because of sex or race know that they will never be more female or more black, or more of whatever their distinguishing mark may be. But the old face an inevitable increase of the condition for which already they are being belittled, excluded and pushed aside.

[*78*]

As this realization grasped me, I found myself suddenly sick with fear. The future had always been my refuge—a place of safety to work toward. No matter how bad my problems had got, the future had always been the promised land, where those problems would be solved. I looked forward in confidence and hope. Tomorrow would be better. But now that my problems stemmed from being old, I could only expect my tomorrows to get increasingly worse. I felt surrounded by walls that were closing in. The future was gone! And I did not know how to live without a better tomorrow beckoning me on. I could only hide my face.

Oasis in the Desert

Suddenly everything in my world had a different appearance. The discovery that I was old demanded a change in my conception of how others saw me, as well as how I saw myself and my future. Overloaded already with adjustments, I couldn't meet these new requirements head-on. I had to find a way of escape.

Escape is currently a dirty word. Hiding from a problem is what many people consider cowardice. Once I would have agreed. But now I felt that for anyone about to be shredded by a lion or a bear—or a problem—the first order of business is to get away. Otherwise there will be nothing left to seek a braver solution. As old age and ageism towered ferociously over me, I fled headlong in search of some quiet, lovely place where I could hide and rest. I needed to be alone with nature and let my healing come through her.

I had been reared on a large farm where the natural creation overwhelmed the senses, where man and his emanations were only a tiny portion of the rest. I had slept with the soft sound of rustling leaves, and the staccato beat, gentle patter and muffled thud of rain on roof and trees and ground. Mornings, the fresh smell of new growth greeted me. Even after I married and left the farm, I lived within a glorious view of the Blue Ridge Mountains. I was used to woods, fields, streams, and rolling hills. Deep in my ears and very bones still lingered an echo of the songs of birds, the hum and chirrup of insects, and the fascinating cries of animals, wild and domestic, calling to one another in their diverse tongues.

In my new surroundings, the sights, sounds, and odors of an artificial lifestyle invaded the memories of the natural world my body still retained. The trees at my windows helped, but they were only token nature. I could almost feel their repressed tears of loneliness as they faced apartment houses, office buildings, and the great asphalt highway across the parking lot. Beneath their slowly swaying branches human voices and faces, alien in their tension, could be heard and seen. And round these taut persons, like a swarm of gnats, a profusion of small litter fanned out—match folders, candy and chewing gum wrappers, empty cigarette packages, used tissues. I needed a place of rest from all this.

I looked for a retreat beyond the urban clutter. But on the highway leading out, a seemingly endless drizzle of construction met me—high rises interspersed with filling stations, shopping centers, and buildings being raised or razed. Occasionally I glimpsed in the distance a wooded hill and eagerly drove there, only to find a new array of construction machinery busily gouging out trees. Nothing seemed left of the kind of country I longed for.

True, there were nearby parks. But when I looked at them I found that in the thirty years since I had visited such places, the throw-away culture and the high cost of labor had joined hands to create a horrifying result. Almost every small article and snack from nearby stores came in some disposable container that most people, regardless of where they opened it, simply let fall at their feet. No longer to be seen was the once familiar figure of a man with a spiked stick and huge canvas bag busily spearing litter and pushing it into his widemouthed sack. Wherever I went, there was the sound of traffic or construction or canned rock music from buildings, cars, or pocket radios.

I resorted to walks at dawn when nature is at her freshest and human pollution at its least. One morning as the sun crept up, I decided to explore a gorge that lay on the other side of the highway between the shopping center parking lot and a large area used by the county for dumping leaves. It looked unpromising, but treetops protruded from it and the dumped leaves on one side, plus the big parking lot on the other side removed the gorge a bit from the worst noises of artificial life.

As I neared the gorge's edge, I was not surprised to see the usual signs of human visitation surrounding the steep path leading down—beer cans, broken bottles, paper bags, plastic cups, soggy newspapers, even an occasional rotting garment. Repelled, I hesitated. But the sound of gurgling water pulled me on. I pushed through a curtain of scraggly bushes, and struggled and clutched my way down the uneven, precipitous path.

Then suddenly, as though a door had opened, I came upon a green glade and a few steps farther on—a gravel beach. Beyond the beach a stream eight feet wide swept over large rocks and poured down into a still, clear pool, then tumbled out again in rapids. Across the stream, facing me, a huge rock rose almost straight up in a thirty-foot cliff laced with bright green moss. Overhead darker green foliage stirred. Birds fluttered among the branches. Squirrels moved in their characteristic little jerks.

I sank to the ground with a slow, deep breath. If only I were still for a while, I thought, surely the birds would sing. But even if they didn't, there were the whispers of wind brushing leaves against each other and the gay, swift, unhurried sound of water dancing its way toward the sea! The depth of the ravine and the thick curtain of foliage above combined to conceal the ugly sounds and sights outside. Even at midday this probably was a quiet place. In the early morning it was like a mountain pass.

But the illusion of remoteness fell away when my eyes strayed from the cliff and stream and trees to the mess around me. The debris here was as bad as it was at the entrance to the path. Untidy picnickers had left a long accumulation of fruit skins, napkins, sandwich bags, plastic containers, bottles, and cans. Even an old paperback book had been forgotten and lay, rain soaked and rotting, in the damp earth.

I didn't intend, however, to discard this genuine jewel merely because of a shabby setting. The setting could be changed. Seizing the largest bag I saw among the litter, I stuffed it with other trash, then filled another and another and another. By the time the sun was hot, the water's edge for thirty feet, a short strip of beach, and part of the grassy bank had an almost unspoiled look. Damp and panting, I sank on a fallen tree trunk and drank the smell and touch and sight of nature—earth and leaves, wild blossoms and water. There was even a wild huckleberry bush. I reveled in the berries' cool, firm little bodies and tangy taste. Surely all our senses were made for knowing nature, not for the queer, confusing concoctions we ourselves produce.

How entrancing was the wild water's swish and tinkle as it dealt with all the obstacles in its path. How good and clean and homelike was the unadulerated sound of many leaves consorting in the breeze. After a long, slow time I rose, shining within. One by one, I carried my bulging trash bags up the steep bank and left them in the supermarket's bins. Then in peace and curious inner comfort, I sauntered back across the highway bridge.

The next morning I could hardly wait to get to my oasis. I expected to find my accomplishment of the day before at least half undone. It wasn't so. In less than a minute I gathered up the can or two and other bits of trash that had appeared in my clean areas since yesterday. Then I was free to redeem new ground. This time I had brought large trash bags from home. They made my task easier for my apartment-bound muscles, which now were getting sore.

It took almost two weeks of daily labor to remove the accumulated junk. But what remained when I had finished was a glorious retreat only a five-minute walk from home. And once the initial collection was cleared away, the place was no harder to keep neat than one's own back yard might be if it were blessedly frequented with cookouts and kids.

My oasis brought me a feeling of ownership. I needed it to offset my growing sense of rootlessness. All my life I had owned a piece of earth. Everywhere that my short legs took me as a child was on our land. My father and grandfather were born there. It was almost as if I had grown out of the land. Now I owned nothing. Or rather, until I found my oasis, this was true. But for all practical purposes at dawn each day this mountain pass retreat was altogether mine. My very body knew it, for my muscles told it so.

What is ownership? I think it rests chiefly in such things as love, involvement and responsibility. If we love a place, if our longings and satisfactions are arranged around it, and if we make ourselves responsible for its upkeep, even though someone else may own the deed, deep within us true ownership is ours.

My oasis also gave me the good knowledge that others besides myself gained by my toil. Picnickers and lovers must take more pleasure in surroundings that were clean and fresh. I even hoped that some of them delighted in the place as I did—and left no litter because they found none.

Then there was the fact that the work entailed bending and twisting, carrying and climbing. I stretched and strengthened muscles I had not used since my own yard and garden claimed my care. I liked feeling limber and strong again.

In addition to all that, the experience taught me a useful lesson. To most of us it appears to be a futile task to make oneself responsible for keeping public places clean. But in fact it's rather easy. It appears hopeless only because of the long build-up that results when no one tries to keep them clean. Once the accumulation is removed, maintenance isn't hard at all.

After my success with my oasis, I adopted the littered parking lot beneath my bedroom window. Men working on their cars in the evenings and on weekends left greasy rags, empty oil cans, junk-food wrappers, and even an occasional whole newspaper, which when caught by the wind would distribute itself widely. But compared to the litter-encrusted oasis, trash in the parking lot was very thinly spread. An investment of less than an hour sufficed for me to clean it up the first time, and after that an average of a dozen new throwaways a day was all I had to gather.

Some of the other tenants thought that only a fool would be a wageless trash collector. One or two politely said so. But I knew otherwise. Already I had reaped the fruits of my wisdom. I felt *good* that two small areas of my world were pleasanter for everybody because of me. In the thirteen years since then, I have persisted in redeeming the parking lot from a disgrace to a respectable car port. An average of two minutes—one hundred-twenty seconds!—a day is all it takes. In investing my muscles and minutes by improving public places, the reward lies in learning that great changes *can* follow little work.

"I live here," I remind each new critic. "It's my home. And it's fun to try to make it nicer for us all."

Maybe I have won some converts by such talk. I know the lot is getting easier to keep clean. Besides the people who drop less litter, I suspect that some also secretly pick it up.

But whether or not my public works influence others, they influence me. Anywhere I find myself waiting, I am likely to begin a public work. Once in a nearby laundromat, I caught myself criticizing how the place was kept. An absent, lazy or over-worked janitor never bothered to wipe away the blend of spilled detergent and dust that clung to every ledge of the nice, white washers.

"Well," I thought, "here you stand loafing while you wait. So whose fault is it if the washers aren't clean?"

I retrieved a scrub cloth from my sudsy hot water

and did a thorough job on the machine I was using. One week later when I returned, the machine I had scrubbed was startlingly cleaner than the rest. So I was hooked. I washed them all. In the following months I found that it took only five minutes or so once a week to keep them quite presentable. When public places become dismal, it's because not one person undertakes to clean them up.

I'm grateful that my oasis lured me into the wisdom, comfort, and pleasure of giving away my drudgery. This habit is a lifeline that helps me to feel I pull my weight, small as my contributions often are. Sometimes, even, they aren't so small. I noticed one day that poison ivy was spreading rapidly under our numerous shrubs. I reported it to the management but nothing was done about it. Perhaps the maintenance men, city-bred, could not tell this attractive looking vine from such welcome ground covers as Virginia creeper. I put on rubber gloves, pulled up the menace root by root, stuffed it in plastic bags, and sent it off with the trash. It took less than an hour. Yet each time I see children playing under those now-safe shrubs, I have the lovely warmth of knowing that they are safe because of me.

Through all the quicksand and bewilderment I was soon to traverse before I found firm ground and good solutions, I knew my oasis was there, always the same, always waiting and dependable. And I knew that the lessons it taught me were dependable, too. These small certainties held steady when all else seemed to fall away. It may have saved me from a breakdown.

Yet, by itself, it was not enough. The oasis was a place of solitude and rest. But I needed interaction, too. I needed fellowship and the close relationships that grow when people work together for a common goal. So after a few months of catching my breath from the spinning shock of learning I was old, my first emotion was gratitude for my church.

No Hiding Place

In all the stark strangeness of knowing that my future would now be dictated by old age, I also knew that within the body of Christ I was protected by enduring concepts of what it means to be a child of God. No matter how dislocating and destructive the months and years ahead might be, in the home and family of my church I would have an area of solidity, permanence, strength and eternal belonging. Resting in the shared worship of an unchanging person, my outside losses would be cushioned, and I could handle the wrenching changes in my body and outer life.

Even more important, no matter what happened to me, in my church family I would always have something of value to give. In secular society, the old often are left with nothing to contribute. They are expected merely to receive. Yet without something to give, human creatures can experience themselves only as half-persons. Of that condition I felt great fear. But as long as I could share my inner life with my church family, I need not have that foreboding. Regardless of our physical condition and material circumstances, within the body of Christ we can give our unique vision and experience of the pearl-with-out-price. Under stress, suffering, losses and death, we can still offer to persons who know its value our unique knowledge of God's special caring for us. And isn't this gift the foundation of security, hope, courage, and love, both for the one who gives and the one who receives it?

With my need for my church family so large, my vulnerability to their human shortcomings was also large. Most serious Christians, I think, consciously try hard to be kind and thoughtful. But in a culture that brainwashes us all into holding certain stereotypes without our knowing that we hold them, most of us need consciousness raising as well as good intentions. There are many ways in which well-meaning people discount the old without even suspecting that is what they are doing.

For instance, a TV evangelist exhorted his viewers on a national network, "Give your life to Jesus while you're young! Don't wait till you're old and he can't do anything with you!"

Doubtless he would have been shocked had he realized the brutal implication that even God has no uses for the old. Yet he voiced that message, and it rolled out into thousands of old ears, many of whose owners must have been listening in the hope of receiving comfort.

About the same time, the Pope announced his decision that cardinals over the age of eighty could no longer vote in papal elections. The obvious assumption was that, regardless of the amount of knowledge, training, experience and dedication a loyal servant of God might have, when he is old, his Lord no longer guides his judgment in the service of the church he loves. Even though I happen to be Protestant, the

Pope's announcement fell heavily on my heart.

In my own denomination, the minister of one of the largest churches in the Washington area stated in a lecture series that when he first took over his present parish, he tried to shock the old people in his flock into leaving. This had seemed to him a sensible first step in revitalizing the church. "But now I'm glad they didn't all go," he added with the air of a man offering both good news and a radical discovery. "Because some of them do have something on the ball." From the wounded fawn look in the eyes of several other old people present, I gathered that they, too, had gotten the message that even the church considers them a liability.

At the time, I literally could not believe my ears. It seemed impossible that a minister of the gospel would be so brutal as to do what he said he had done and so rude as to tell about it in a meeting where one in six of his listeners was old. I later learned that a frequent stereotype held by young clergymen is of old people as the fat cats of the church, powerful and set in their ways, leaning back in their comfortable pews, running the church and obstructing all progress. It was supposed to require great strength and courage for a minister to stand firm against them.

While that wound still ached, Bebe Walker, a prominent member of St. Luke's, telephoned to say she would like to take me to a big church luncheon. I felt comforted by her friendly outreach and accepted gratefully. Then I added that since I had my own car, I could meet her there and save her having to pick me up and take me home.

A little shock of pleasure ran through me when she insisted: "No, let me come and get you. Then we can talk going to and coming from the church, as well as at lunch. Ever since you first came to St. Luke's, I've wanted to know you better."

But I was hardly settled in Bebe's car when I knew she had no real interest in me. She pelted me with routine questions—"When did you come to Arlington? . . . Do you like it here? . . . Have you read any good books lately?"—but she listened to none of my answers. Instead, she muttered at traffic, remarked on the weather, and pointed out landmarks as I tried to reply. In regard to how I liked it here, my answer included the fact that I loved my apartment and its window trees. Five minutes later she asked, "Do you like your apartment?"

At the luncheon, she addressed herself almost entirely to persons on her other side and across the narrow table. I fought a losing battle against the obvious conclusion that she had asked me only as a Christian duty. My worst heartaches were confirmed a few weeks later when she appeared at another luncheon with another elderly woman in tow, who looked as ignored and miserable as I had felt. It was a long time before I recovered enough to experience again a small shock of pleasure when anyone expressed a wish to know me better.

I know that Bebe's intentions were good. She was trying to be-kind-to-*oldpeople*. But if there are people, old or young, who want to be objects of kindness, I haven't met them. What we want and need is recognition and welcoming. This must be given "without partiality," for group distinctions have no place in God's mind (James 2:1; Gal. 3:28).

Having long believed that the purpose of bitter experiences is to learn from them, I examined mine for lessons. But the time was not yet ripe. I netted only confusion. So I pushed them into a mental closet and focused on gratitude for the good things that still abounded. Among these were Joe and Sue Lox. I felt secure in our closeness. They seemed to enjoy me, to care about me as a person, and to regard me as an important church member.

Joe often reminded me that he counted on me to help with church renewal. As that phrase was bounced around by him and his guest speakers, I began to wonder if I fully grasped what they meant by it. But surely they meant deepening and stimulating faith that tended to become shallow and routine. This we all needed. New approaches to worship and Christian education would be included. But although I loved our services as they were, I favored any omissions, additions and changes in wording that would help us see and hear the rich, eternally true messages of our faith with fresh eyes and ears.

At Joe's suggestion, I enrolled in a weekend workshop on how to create new liturgies. I found it fascinating and clarifying. Joe was delighted by my enthusiasm and my efforts to sell the idea of experimental liturgies to less flexible members of the parish. But renewal would involve more than that. I wanted to learn all I could. I was first in line for a ticket to a widely publicized four-hour workshop on "Christian Renewal in Today's Culture."

The seminar was being sponsored by a well-known church in the District. The leader was a professor at a distinguished university and was renowned as an exciting workshop leader. I slipped into my seat on a chilly, rainy Saturday and waited eagerly for the workshop to begin. I felt good. Now that I had taken hold of my problems instead of being overwhelmed by them, I had lost most of my recent, heavy fear of the future. Again I was plowing in hope, and some of my old, excited anticipation of challenge had returned.

Our leader, Dr. Trigg (as I'll call him, though that isn't his name) was a vigorous, intellectually agile man in early middle life. Hurling himself like a baseball into his topic, he began by saying that Christians today must learn to approach all people with a kind of reverence simply because they are persons.

"Persons are made in the image of God. This means they need no other qualification to be of ultimate value. Deep, unswerving respect is due each, regardless of his cultural, educational, or economic status, and of his natural endowments."

He went on to stress that even when the person has subnormal intelligence, undeveloped conscience and repellent personal characteristics, agape love, God's kind of love, is due him just because he is a person. In giving him this love we ourselves are made whole. Indeed, our own wholeness as persons depends on a kind of human fellowship that knows no boundaries whatever.

My spirit began to soar. How beautifully he perceived and expressed the very truths I had been experiencing so sharply and inarticulately. I wondered where he learned how it feels not to be accorded the dignity of full personhood. No wonder he was famous. His tenderness and respect for people who are so ungifted and untrained that they have only their personhood to offer shone through his terse, apt phrasing. He cared about those stripped-down persons he was talking about. I was deeply moved and I think the other listeners were, too. Had the workshop ended there, I would have been left with the enormous treasure of feeling more able to love.

But following the first lecture and coffee break, a change in his message and attitude was evident.

"To this point in the theological landscape, traditional Christians move comfortably on firm ground," he said brusquely. "But beyond this point, what they consider solid doctrine is seen by intelligent modern theologians as no better than a bog. Traditional Christianity is neither relevant nor applicable to modern life. Its total collapse is a mark of our time. If Christianity is to survive as an important influence, we must change our way of thinking and talking about God, religion, and the church."

I was astonished. My own experience was the reverse. After struggling for two-thirds of my life to manage without traditional Christianity, I had concluded that it was the most relevant and applicable force anywhere.

"Science has made the concept of a transcendent, personal God unbelievable for an educated person," Dr. Trigg continued. "The only possible religion for intelligent people today is a religion simply of acts of kindness and justice. In the Bible God himself tells us to stop worshiping him and serve our fellow men."

Here he quoted Amos's famous passage in chapter 5, verses 21-24, where God demands that justice be substituted for "solemn assemblies"; St. James's warning in 1:27 that true religion requires visiting orphans and widows (though Dr. Trigg omitted "to keep oneself unstained from the world"); and Jesus's statement in Mark 2:27, "The sabbath was made for man, not man for the sabbath."

In context I thought the message of these passages

was plainly that our transcendant, personal God demands that we *worship him by loving and serving his children.* That is quite different from taking God out of the picture and putting people in the center of it!

"Some people cling to the old concept of God to make them feel safe and secure." Dr. Trigg thrust those two words out with a force that implied that any wish to have either of these feelings was highly culpable. I didn't see why. "We lean on the Ten Commandments as an easy way out of making moral decisions." I didn't see them as easy. "In making moral decisions we must assume that we may be making the worst possible choices rather than choosing the right. An honest Christian isn't sure of anything." Being sure of the love and goodness of God was essential to my ability both to risk and to contend. I did not think I could function adequately with the cast of mind Dr. Trigg now was insisting on. Yet in his first talk he had been so magnificently right. My thoughts began to career dizzily.

A second coffee break followed lecture number two, and when it was over Dr. Trigg seated himself for the question period with an amiable smile. "Give full expression to your thoughts and feelings, please," he said. "Then I'll learn, too. Some of you must disagree. Let's hear how and why."

Several people asked for clarification of various points. Others commented on points they thought interesting.

"Oh, come now!" he protested. "You're not challenging me. Who disagrees with what I said?"

"I do," I told him. "Traditional Christianity seems to speak to basic human needs too directly for it to be inapplicable in these or any other times. It meets my own deepest needs constantly—when nothing else does."

Fixing his eyes on a corner of the ceiling, Dr. Trigg replied in a tone of half-amused annoyance.

"Only people who are unable—physically, intellectually, or emotionally—to face real issues are likely to agree with you, I'm afraid. There's a great difference between what we need and what we want. Children want candy, but they need entirely different food. We may hold to traditional Christianity, but we need to be kicked off our knees and into action in the world."

A young clergyman stood up. "How could a faith that has been an inspiration for nearly two thousand years, and to which many great men acknowledge a debt, suddenly become irrelevant in one generation? If we have lost our sense of the reality of God, maybe it's because we don't pray enough. If we ignore God, naturally we become unaware of him. So how can ignoring him even further cure our situation?"

Dr. Trigg examined his fingernails, smiling. "I confess the value of prayer eludes me. In a science-oriented culture, the conception of God as the man upstairs who can be called down by raising your voice is pretty ridiculous, don't you think? What we need is an honest, workable faith that an educated man can accept."

"Dr. Trigg," interposed a tiny, frail woman of about seventy-five, "when I pray, God is right there, as real as any friend. More real than some. If you don't pray, you don't know what comfort you're missing."

"I'll let you pray for me," he replied with a condescending chuckle. "But please don't pray that

I'll find 'comfort'. I've gotten past the thumb-sucking stage. . . . Who's next?"

By the end of the seminar I felt as I once had felt after a midnight drive through a part of town that I had seen only during busy hours. The buildings and streets were there, but they were lonely-looking and bare. Dr. Trigg's version of Christianity and the Bible were not recognizable to me as the faith and book I knew.

The Rock Crumbles

When I woke next morning, the dawn was gray.
Emptiness reached out around me like the emptiness of a desert or an open sea. I felt indescribable isolation, as prisoners may feel in solitary confinement or as old people may feel upon learning of the death of the last person who loved them. I rose more weary than when I went to bed and dragged myself through my bath and preparation for breakfast.

I had been curiously exhausted yesterday when the seminar was over. I felt not just tired but spent. Finished, almost. That made no sense! True, my encounter with Dr. Trigg was painful. After his beautiful affirmation of the importance of personhood in his first talk, he had roughly discounted the personhood of all of us who disagreed with his position. But that was his problem. I shouldn't take it personally.

As for his intimations that my sedentary life, my lack of natural endowments, and my emotional immaturity had made me choose an all-day-sucker type of Christianity, I knew he had missed the mark. During the black revolution, when I had battled on the minority side of what was then the nation's hottest issue, a stream of threats and insults had descended on me that only my faith had enabled me to survive. Traditional Christianity had been for me no candy bar but the staff of life.

Dr. Trigg must be unaware of how he sounded. With his declared respect for all persons, he surely wouldn't knowingly be contemptuous of the pillars of a fellow Christian's faith. He sounded almost as though—here something deep in me reached back into bitter past experience and began to ache like a broken bone—as though if we didn't see Christianity as he did, we were less than human, therefore not persons. His smilingly condescending dismissal of our beliefs reminded me of certain convinced segregationists I had known who saw people who disagreed with them as less than persons and not entitled to any respect whatever.

So why didn't I just shrug the workshop off as unproductive for me and turn my attention to something more fruitful? I found I could not. My mind went round and round in the experience as though it held some hidden significance for me. Could it be that Dr. Trigg was so sure of himself that it seemed *he must know of strong support for his views throughout the church?* Such a stab of pain went through me at the thought that my mind veered off from the question.

My eyes fell on the clock. If I hurried I had just time to make the eight o'clock Communion service. I felt miraculously eased at the prospect. I speedily dressed and ran downstairs and across the parking lot to my car. Maybe I could talk to Joe after the service. I wanted his sympathy and reassurance.

Everything began going my way. The day was

sparklingly clear after its gray beginning and the drizzly rain of yesterday; the beautiful, deep affirmations of the service filled me with a sense of belonging, strength and quiet joy; friends seemed to greet me with special warmth; and as I moved into the parish hall after the service, Joe joined me and asked how I liked the seminar, adding:

"You were the lucky one. Nobody else I know learned about it in time to get a ticket."

"Lucky!!!" I poured out my distress.

As I talked, Joe's face stiffened, his eyes became remote. I thought he was identifying with me until he spoke. "Patty, I'm disappointed. You make me wonder why you stick around with me. I think Dr. Trigg's terrific—the most exciting of the young theologians. And they're an exciting bunch. By me, he has the answers to how to save the church. But nothing can save her if she won't listen. I thought you wanted renewal."

"I do, Joe. Heaven knows the church needs more commitment. But I don't call undermining the foundations renewal. You don't renew a building by tearing it down. Dr. Trigg seems to want to junk some of the essential features of Christianity."

"Like what?"

"Like a personal God who loves us and listens to us."

Joe looked into my eyes without sympathy. "I can't help you," he said. "Why don't you think about what Dr. Trigg said and what I've been saying ever since you came to St. Luke's? Maybe you can see sense in the new solutions. I'll tell you one thing: it's those or nothing! They're the only solutions we've got for a dying church." He turned abruptly and walked away.

Years later, when the theological emphasis shifted

once more, I was to learn that any sharp turn in the direction of the church's thrust tends to bring with it an almost fanatical conviction that the new direction offers the sole hope of survival. The result is that certain beliefs become idols, and various kinds of human sacrifice to them are made. Had I known that then, I might have been a little more objective about what was happening to me.

At that time, I knew only that never before had Joe spoken to me like that—as if my agreeing with him was more important than I was. It chilled me to the bone. As with Dr. Trigg, I seemed to have disqualified myself as a human being in his eyes by defending traditional Christianity! It was as though he felt I had declared myself an enemy of the true faith, and therefore had become his enemy. But if Joe believed what Dr. Trigg believed, how could I have failed to see it?

A few minutes after my exchange with Joe, I found myself standing next to Sue, as we both exclaimed over the youngest member of our congregation, who was snuggled, sleeping, against his pretty mother. After a moment Sue turned to me and asked:

"How was the seminar?"

Assuming that Joe's anger stemmed in part from my giving him the false impression that I saw value in nothing Dr. Trigg had said, I picked my way carefully. I told Sue how marvelous his first talk had been, and only then added that later I was shaken by his rejection of prayer and of God as a person.

Sue's face, alight with interest when I began, grew slowly inscrutable, flat-eyed, withdrawn. "I'm sorry you were disappointed," she said coldly. "I'd have given anything to hear him."

"You don't agree with him about prayer, do you?" I asked, confident of a denial.

Her eyes were grave and steady as she answered. "I think I do—now. My old beliefs are beginning to seem kind of stuffy to me. The new approaches free us from a bunch of junk we've been carrying around. Life will be much more fun when we throw the old stuff away. Don't you really think so?"

"I think it will be less fun," I said, "and more meaningless."

"Then, my dear, you just keep right on believing as you always have," she advised me primly, reaching out and giving my cheek a little pat. If she had added the words "great-grandmother," her thought couldn't have been plainer.

At the time, I was staggered by meeting again in Joe and Sue the personal hostility I had endured from Dr. Trigg. Although the memory still smarts today, at least now I'm not bewildered. I know that during the 1960s many seminaries heavily stressed the value of righteous indignation. The earlier gentle Jesus model was viewed with passionate distaste. The conviction flourished that spineless, sentimental interpretations of Christianity must be forcefully uprooted to make room for a more virile and honest faith.

Add to that the belief, widespread and vigorous at the time, that only through a radically new interpretation of scriptures and doctrines could Christianity possibly survive in our scientific age. Add also the stereotype of old people as complacently powerful in the church and fiercely defensive of their comfortable pew. When all these elements are put together, the picture suddenly rounds out. The hostility I and others suffered from some churchmen begins to make sense. They saw old people as wolves rather than as sheep. Their harsh treatment of the "entrenched old guard" seemed to them a brave defense of the faith against a snarling threat.

But I lacked those clues to ecclesiastical thinking at the time I was being slugged by it. I knew only that my collision with Dr. Trigg, Joe and Sue left me confounded. After my exchange with the Loxes, I returned home at once and spent the rest of the morning trying to make sense of it all.

The feelings of emptiness and isolation that had oppressed me when I first woke that morning now returned reinforced, sweeping over me in sick waves. And through them all I felt the heavy pulse and suck of fear. I felt trapped, lonely, and full of despair. And for the first time, I felt truly old.

It was now several months since I had recognized that I was old. But shocked as I had been at first, I had not felt old. Now I did. It wasn't a feeling of accumulated years so much as one of having outlived my power to achieve anything—a feeling of not having any life ahead of me but only behind me, of having passed from anticipation into merely marking time. There wasn't anything out there for me—no adventure, or fulfillment, or unlived life, or accomplishment. There would only be more and more of the same, more and more old age, more and more losses, more and more becoming an outsider, even in my church family.

My mind was flooded with biblical images that expressed symbolically what I could not yet say in words. I saw myself being left, huddled alone, beside a trail through a wilderness while the caravan of my people moved on without anyone glancing back. Then, in another sequence, I saw myself watching from the wall of what I had believed to be an impregnable fortress the approach of an over-whelming army. And even as I resolved to fight, I knew that the walls would fall.

My symbolic images had the unoriginality and quality of emotion often found in nightmares. A feeling of hopelessness, of total defeat, clung to them. My heart knew their meaning. The first one meant that the church was all I had left to enable me to grapple with the predicament of old age, and that the church was now dumping me on the roadside because they thought my kind of Christianity only hampered growth in the new church. The second one meant that fight as I would to save my own faith, the forces of today's culture would break it down.

But fight I must. And I would need ammunition. I must learn when the views voiced by the Loxes and Dr. Trigg developed in the church and if they were widespread. Faint memories stirred just below the surface of my consciousness like an army moving in the dark. I had an uneasy feeling that I had long been hearing those views from the pulpit, without grasping their import.

That their real meaning had passed me by wasn't strange. I had fallen into the common error of hearing ministers say what I assumed they believed. My own experience in public speaking should have taught me that people often interpret what they hear in terms of what they expect to hear. From the pulpit especially, where even the newest messages tend to be couched in the familiar words and phrases of tradition, listeners often miss the newness and hear only what the old words call to mind. Not suspecting that my church might not be teaching traditional interpretations of our faith, I had filtered out anything contrary to traditional beliefs.

Months later, after playing over tapes of some of Joe's old sermons, I could hear what indeed he had been saying all along. The mysterious extra dimension I had attributed to what he said was merely my interpretation of the gap between what I had thought he must be saying and what he actually meant.

I had heard messages from Joe that he didn't intend, partly because his sermons were richly sprinkled with the kind of phrasing that quickens a committed Christian's pulse. Listening to the tapes, I listed traditional words he often used. Then I asked Joe what he meant by them. Here are some of his replies:

"By *God* I mean the power we all have for facing difficulties in our lives. . . . To me *Christ* is a function—the way we receive new experience. . . . *Salvation* is being helped in any moment of jeopardy. If a friend saves me from drowning or from breaking my leg, that is salvation. . . . *Prayer* is giving public expression to my concern. I don't expect an answer. And I don't think there's anything on the other end hearing me."

But, as I said, that information I gathered later. On this Sunday afternoon, I knew only that nothing happening to me seemed to make any sense. I had to know more about what was going on in the national church. I would search in the periodical room of the public library for all religious news during the last several years. The library opened at one o'clock on Sundays. I was there waiting when the doors were unlocked. By closing time, five hours later, my worst suspicions were confirmed.

This happened only a few weeks before the God-Is-Dead slogan became headline news in April 1966. The groundwork that resulted in the slogan had already been laid. Theologians, religion teachers, and prominent clergymen who made news announced that secularism was the "in" thing. The idea of a transcendent God was "out." If traditional Christianity was anywhere being plugged by churchmen, reporters didn't think the fact worth mentioning.

No wonder when Dr. Trigg attacked traditional beliefs he was so ominously sure of his ground that he did not even bother to choose his words carefully or to explain shades of meaning. He well knew his position was supported by the majority of his colleagues. More courage was required to defend traditional Christianity during the God-Is-Dead era than to scoff at it!

Feelings of helplessness throbbed painfully in me. I wanted to fight for what had made life lovely and purposeful for me. But the gap was too wide between my passionate, clear-cut feelings and my intellectual grasp of what was happening in the church. I could not make sense of it. All I could do was smart and ache, feel empty and lost. Without recognizable warning, a new set of norms and rules for living had been established. Christian lay people were being rebuked and discounted by clergymen and theologians of our own denomination for beliefs that the church herself had taught us only a generation ago. We were being psychologically pistol-whipped for maintaining theological postures and ethical standards that had been drilled into us as essential to the Christian life.

I didn't know then what surveys and experiments

have since shown in scientific research, that people and animals alike tend to break down when behavior from which they have always gotten pleasure begins consistently to produce pain. I only knew that in the one area of my life where I had felt totally sure I belonged, almost overnight I had become a hopeless outsider. Mores, values, doctrines, and morals had become, without my suspecting it, different from those I had been taught. Nearly everything I believed essential in the Christian faith was, in the eyes of persons I looked to for authority and guidance, obsolete and unacceptable.

The news of religion for the past several years was that the ten commandments had become "the ten suggestions" and were being replaced rapidly by situation ethics. The voice of conscience was now seen as one's inner parent issuing dubious demands. Religious expression was being called "religiosity." Morals were dubbed "moralistic" or "legalistic." Worship and prayer were referred to as "pietistic." Basic doctrines were designated simplistic.

I felt betrayed by the church. In my dissolving inner world, I desperately needed to hear firm voices proclaim enduring truths and to grasp the strong hands of centuries-old convictions. Without the help of the church, there was no shelter I could creep into as darkness deepened on the vast desert where I now stood shivering alone.

Deep inside me I felt the seething of repressed anger as my courage, emotional health, and hope crumpled under the impact of the blows they had received in the months since, full of faith, confidence, and anticipation, I had moved toward a new life. I knew I needed at least one area of continuity, stability, and acceptance of me as a child of God, or I would surely fall apart. It was hard to forgive my church for not supplying that need.

In the wake of the anger came a sense of guilt. "I should be grateful," I told myself, "for the fact that people want to be kind to me. Certainly I should be grateful to our church leaders for their honesty in not claiming beliefs they no longer hold."

But gratitude for grinding pain is not easily acquired. As I struggled to repress my anger, no gratefulness took its place. Instead, dense depression settled in.

A Little Less than Human

F ollowing the experiences described in the last two chapters, I began a four-year losing battle to maintain a healthy sense of self-worth, of personhood and, above all, of being a child of God. My thoughts obediently repeated appropriate affirmations, but my heart seemed unable to respond.

Little or no help came from outside. I looked and listened in vain for intimations from any quarter that the old have anything to contribute to anyone or any task. Yet low-rating the old is a new stance in the world. Until a generation ago, the old were taken more seriously than the young. To that fact a collection of handed-down laws eloquently attests. To serve a long array of public offices, even to exercise a long list of freedoms—such as voting, driving, drinking, marrying, to name only a few—the law firmly states that we must have reached a certain age. Not until quite recent years has any cut-off age for either offices or freedoms even been discussed.

Two generations ago literature and drama bristled with premises and implications that aging brings assets. Daily social contacts and even advertisements reflected that assumption. Among the universally conceded assets of the old have been wisdom, stability, reliability, mellowness, patience, understanding, temperance, gentleness, experience, better judgment, and a keener sense of moral values and of proportion. Little remains of that view now. The once constantly used phrase "older and wiser heads" is heard no more. "Younger is better" is taken for granted. My ears rang now with such phrases as "old fogies," "old fossils," and "the unretired senile." (By now, senile was used as a synonym for demented.) On all sides the mandatory retirement age, like a broken record, continually repeated the message that we old—regardless of the quality of our natural gifts and accumulated experience—were only a liability to society and to the work force. (Since the time covered by this chapter, legislation has been passed requiring that the mandatory retirement age in some cases be pushed from sixty-five to seventy—an encouraging first step in the right direction.)

It is curious how little aware of these deadly messages I had been until I learned that I myself was old. Then I was shocked to find how loaded our culture is with reiterations that we old deserve the exclusions we suffer, and that there's nothing unjust about them. For example, a man being interviewed on television concerning the need to reorganize certain institutions offered this opinion:

"The trouble is that most of them have hired retirees to run them—old has-beens that nobody else wants. If we just get rid of the deadwood, these institutions will function as they should." The message here is that hiring the retired will doom projects.

Even a political advertisement, aimed at showing how concerned for all people the candidate was, stated gravely: "He listens to the young, who can see things freshly; he listens to the old talk about their problems." Could the implication be clearer that the old have nothing but problems to contribute to our society?

Now that I had become fully aware of the process of stereotyping, then segregating, then discounting, then blanking out the old, I was staggered by how all-inclusive and relentless this process is. As a brainwashing technique, it could not have been more effective had it been designed and executed by some mastermind. In the late 1960s and early 1970s, even the fashions passed along the message that the time had come simply to wipe away the old, as though from a blackboard with a wet sponge.

Earlier in the century, every clothing store and fashion book featured selections designed especially for older people. These selections were considerately created to focus attention on the garment itself, rather than on the body it adorned. But now, low necks and sleeveless bodices, mid-sections designed for trim hips and flat stomachs, and skirts ending halfway between the knee and the groin, all made old people look needlessly unattractive, even ridiculous. It was virtually impossible to find a dress without at least one of the features that cruelly reveal the painful secrets of the old. This fact declared as plainly as if it had been verbalized that most people preferred simply to ignore the fact that old people existed and, like anyone else, needed to have clothes that worked for rather than against them.

To these deadly general messages were added more specific ones from my own experience. For instance, despite the fact that my accident record was faultless, when my birthday rolled round, my automobile insurance premium increased by $80. Smarting with the injustice, I sought another insurance company, only to be quoted still higher rates. When I protested, a kindly salesman frankly advised me not to try to change insurance companies "at your age," explaining that I would find the cards heavily stacked against me.

When I tried still another company, I was told by a less polite salesman, "We're not interested in drivers your age at any premium—no matter how good your record is." There was a steel-like quality in his voice as he added that legislators in some states were considering canceling operator's licenses automatically at age seventy. "I'm in favor of that legislation," he added.

Obviously he was among the many who consider old people a menace on the highway. Yet some recent surveys have shown that the accident rate between ages fifty-five and eighty is lower than in any other comparable age group. I know of at least one insurance company that as a result of that survey, quotes lower, not higher, rates for the old.

A certain quality was missing now from nearly all my relationships. It had to do with togetherness, kinship, and human recognition. Hard to define but not to discern, when this quality is present, we are part of humanity—we belong. When it is absent, we are outsiders, reduced to mere targets of other people's reactions and intentions. This is true whether those reactions and intentions are of protectiveness or exploitation, kindness or hostility. After a while it hardly matters which they are.

I could only guess, for instance, whether that check-out girl in the supermarket mentioned ealier saw herself as protecting me from cigarette dangers, or humoring me in what she supposed my own attitude to be, or poking fun at what she thought was my disapproval. But there was no mistaking the fact that when her eyes fell on me, I suddenly became the object of her condescension. Both "object" and "condescension" are key words here. Condescension always makes an object of its target. And to become an object is always to be dehumanized. It mattered little to me, therefore, whether the girl's own feelings were kindly or not. In either case, she treated me as a nonperson, and thus shoved me toward isolation.

Indeed, becoming an object of kindness can be more painful, and more destructive to human dignity, than becoming an object of hostility—as most members of condescended to minorities will, I think, agree. Perhaps this is because our hearts know that kindness is meant to go hand-in-hand with fellowship, identification and respect. Only so can kindness make the one who receives it feel, not less, but more a person than before.

On the other hand, hostility often jogs our organism automatically into releasing energy for self-defense. This energy can be put to constructive uses if we choose. But condescending kindness leaves us limp and powerless. We can almost feel our knees buckle with weary hopelessness as our sense of personhood begins to wilt. Such condescension says to us, "You're so much less than I that you'll never make it without my help." When that message is repeated and repeated many times by many people in many different ways, confidence that may have been built up through decades of successful achievement begins to fall apart.

It had now been almost five years since, in my sixtieth year, I had moved to my new home. Those years had taught me that the new life I had envisioned was not to be. As the months continued to crawl by, changes had appeared in my habits and attitudes that at first I didn't recognize as ominous. Instead of my accustomed effort to use my time constructively, I began to do anything that would grasp my attention and make me tired enough to sleep. Instead of relaxing with a good book or magazine article, I had to settle for a movie or TV, because I couldn't concentrate on what I read.

In short, no longer did I focus on service and creativity. I only strove to avoid the stalking wolves of fear and pain. Escape from fear and pain became my sole motivation. I was afraid even to think. Thinking might allow the wolves to pounce. And what good could thinking do anyway? I didn't believe solutions to my situation existed.

As I felt myself being pushed from the human race, made an object of stereotyping, of duty, of pity, I found myself becoming (slowly at first, then with acceleration) an object of my own abhorrence. I believed I had nothing to offer anyone. I was sure that people were never nice to me simply because they liked me or wanted to know me better; they were only being kind. And I didn't wonder any more what prompts some old people to say, "Thank you," when they are kissed. Within myself, too, I had become a nonperson.

The earthquake that leveled my once-inviting utopian citadel comprised at least four shocks: the discovery that I was not just getting older but was old already; the realization that the way old people are treated in our culture is even more destructive than the deterioration we all dread; the realization that my lifelong assumption that tomorrow will be better was now for me absurd; and finally, the shattering discovery that there was no safe place I could creep into as my world collapsed—not even the church.

My pain and despair began to have a life of their own. They would draw off and stab me suddenly. They would squeeze my heart until I wanted to beat the wall of my room in sheer agony. They would sink into me until we became one and I was all suffering and hopelessness. They would break away briefly and I would know that any second they would return. They were like hired tormentors—so cunning in their methods that I didn't know which was worse, their presence in me or the sick fear of their return.

I had heard enough about emotional breakdowns to know how close to one I was. Terrified, I began to pray with new urgency that I be spared.

PART II

The Adventure of Recovery

"Out of the Depths"

There is one good thing about despair. It is
rock bottom. Nothing of value is left. So we
can risk anything. We may even be able to let our
securities go—knowing they have failed us. Now we
can seek new securities, or we can reinterpret what
true security is. Despair can drive us to pray in a new
way, resolved to accept any answer that comes. Or
like Jacob, we may wrestle with the angel until he
blesses us.

But all that comes later. At first despair is only
despair. And by its very nature, we see no way out. I
felt betrayed by everything I had depended on. I had
nothing left—no faith, no hope, no love. I still
mouthed the affirmations of my faith. But I couldn't
take them seriously. My church no longer believed
the eternal truths she had taught me. The result was
something that once I would have thought impossible. Other people's lack of faith had never before
undermined my own. I had merely assumed they
didn't yet know what I knew, and I had sought
opportunities to fill them in.

But now the unbelievers were the very persons I
had looked to for guidance and instruction. I had

thought our clergy had chosen the ministry because of deep faith, and that the very nature of their task ensured they would pray more, search scriptures more, and strive more consistently than the rest of us to stay close to God and discern the truth. If such persons could not believe, then perhaps it was true that intelligent, educated people could no longer accept the Christian faith.

It was like hearing an unsavory story about a trusted friend. Faith in him, if real, would not be shaken merely because most people thought him guilty. After all, they didn't know him. But if the members of his immediate family one by one assured his friends that, sad to say, the story was indeed true, they might find it impossible to maintain their trust, despite the pain of its loss.

My pain was so intense I had to do something about it. Necessity is one of the great unappreciated gifts. My whole being was suffocating. My spirit struggled and fought for air. The darkness surrounding me was not the open darkness of night. It was a strangling darkness—like being pushed under the surface of a great black bog. With no hope of an answer, with only the thrust of unlimited pain, I cried out the humblest and most direct of prayers:

"O God! Help me!"

Across my mind flashed an image of the veil of the temple being split. But no lift came in my heaviness. To break the awful silence I switched on my television. A man was being interviewed on a talk show. His firm voice filled the room.

"One of the keys to our recovery," he said, "is a prayer we use. 'God grant me the serenity to accept the things I cannot change, the courage to change the things I can, and the wisdom to know the difference.' "

The message struck like an arrow. I had heard the prayer before. But now I knew it was for me. I believed that if I used it, long-closed doors might open.

"The Serenity Prayer," as it is called, is used by many self-help organizations, the most renowned of which is Alcoholics Anonymous. In this drowning moment, I clutched it—and found it, not a straw, but a tough cord able to pull me out of the depths. With an intensity of interest I had not felt for a long time, I listened to the rest of the interview.

The speaker belonged to one of the many organizations that adapt to problems other than alcohol abuse the twelve-step recovery program developed by AA. The adaptation being offered in this interview was designed for persons suffering from severe emotional pain.

"AA's prayers and guidelines work for us just as they do for alcoholics," the man said. "Our only membership requirement is that you be hurting enough to interfere with your functioning. If you qualify, this prayer will help. But you've got to do more than say it. You've got to act it out."

When the interview was over, I walked to my mirror, looked myself in the eyes and accepted one after another every unacceptable fact that had made quicksand of my life.

"I'm old, wrinkled, gray!" I flung in my face. "I'm defeated, tired, and lost! I've no hope. Old people are just a nuisance today. Even the church sees us as an impediment, not a resource. My faith has wilted and . . . and—yes, it has!—died. I can't believe anymore. I can't trust. I can't care. Every moment of every day all I really want is to die. . . ."

On and on I went, crying out my despair until my

eyes were swollen and red. When I had confessed and accepted each humiliating, terrifying fact, I was quivering, sobbing, and spent.

"That's how it is," I whispered at last. "I accept it."

I stumbled to bed, collapsed, and slept.

I woke once in the night, whispered, "I accept it. Maybe now I can make it my starting place—not my finish . . ." and dozed off again.

When I finally woke, those words were rolling up the shores of my mind like easy breakers on a beach. "My starting place, not my finish! . . . my starting place, my *starting* place." Why, if I had a starting place, I had a *future!* A small piece of firm ground had materialized under my feet. I felt eased and relaxed. Quietness had crept in, even a soft-stepping peace.

Mysteriously, while I slept, this world had become almost mine again. No longer was it a nightmare trap in which I helplessly twisted. True, it wasn't an easy world, but my situation had ceased to be a great boulder pinning me down. I knew it could be the platform on which I stood. Inwardly I rose and went to meet new images of life that were emerging. Once more I could believe that where there's a problem, there's a solution.

Suddenly I realized that the deep, soul-wringing acceptance I had forced upon myself was a positive act! For the first time I had done something definite about my over-all situation. True acceptance is not just giving up! It can be a marshaling of the whole self in the supremely difficult task of taking on a new kind of responsibility—responsibility for how one deals with insufferable experience. I had been trapped in my own attitudes. Now I was being freed from the trap.

Rising from my ashes was not as easy as it sounds

here. Habits of rebellion and hopelessness died hard. I had to repeat my acceptance often. I had to struggle many months before I internalized it and made it part of me. True, from that first, tearful ordeal of acceptance a radical change in my direction took place. No longer was I headed down. I had a goal to work toward, and therefore I had hope. But even now, more than a decade later, when some new intractable obstruction confronts me, I must consciously compel myself to accept it and find another route toward my aims.

It was as though ligaments, nerves, and bones in the intricate body of my faith had been torn and crushed. As with a physical body that has survived a near fatal accident, even when the crisis was passed, my faith could not regain full health at once. Some signs of health were immediate, others lagged. New connections had to be made one by one before living nerves could assume the functions of mangled nerves. When I lifted that despairing prayer, my faith seemed dead. Miraculously, now it was being raised.

Once I had believed that having experienced God moving strongly in my life, I could never doubt again. After knowing his overwhelming presence, doubt seemed impossible. I now know better. Even the great saints and reformers suffered dark nights of the soul when belief seemed naïve. The important thing was that just below the edge of consciousness the love that would not let me go still held me—sometimes sustaining, sometimes haunting, but always there. Even when my faith seemed quite dead, had I not cried out in prayer? Yet the spark of certainty that God was still there—caring and helping—glistened, faded, flashed, and faded again many times before the spark became a flame.

To Change
the Things I Can

After my act of radical acceptance, my energy began to return. I no longer hurled myself against immovable walls. I no longer poured my strength into efforts that could only fail. As a result, my vital forces were available for productive use, and I was ready to change the things I could.

A mountain of needed changes towered over me. Where should I start? With myself! I was the only kit of tools I had, even if they were rusty and dull. With a pencil I listed my most undermining losses of the past five years. The list was long, confusing, overpowering. I pruned and rewrote for hours. Slowly the most devastating losses emerged. Gone was my sense of *progress,* of *contributing,* of *belonging,* and of *loving* and *being loved.*

I decided to start with the sense of progress. It was least dependent on responses of other persons. And once I garnered success with it, I could grapple more confidently with the greater task of achieving success where interaction with others was involved.

A sense of progress is automatic as we grow up. Year by year we become taller, stronger, more independent, better informed. Normally this process continues through middle life. We build up knowledge and experience in our chosen field, earn more, acquire more and better possessions, raise a family, become more established in our community. If a sense of progress is missing in youth or middle age, other persons are sympathetic, and encouragement is given to seek a solution.

In old age, a sense of progress is as necessary for happiness as in youth. But the old are led to believe that progress is not for them, that only deterioration is in store. In such a psychological environment, an experience of progress is achieved only through fierce determination and heroic effort. Yet I had come into the experience of old age with little preparation and few guidelines to help me meet its unique challenges. Where could I look for a sense of progress?

Some of the hobbies and games that are popular with the old offer a sense of progress. Collecting is one. As the collection grows, a feeling of progress grows, too. Searching out the roots and branches of one's family tree is another. Assembling a jigsaw puzzle is briefly effective as one wrests order from chaos. But games and hobbies lacked appeal for me. I wanted my actions to deliver a message that contradicted the one old people too often heard.

I resolved to regain my sense of progress through acquiring new attitudes, new depth of understanding, new knowledge, and new skills. What a relief, what fun it would be to feel again the upward surge of progress! It would be almost like a vacation trip. A long time had passed since I had a vacation. But where should I go for my progress trip?

Excited, I telephoned all the sources of information I could find—the public library, the Department of Recreation, the Adult Education Office, the Chamber of Commerce, the county newspaper. I asked each for a list of low cost opportunities to learn. I found there were many schools, libraries, churches, Y's, museums, government organizations, and even businesses in Arlington that sponsored workshops, training programs, and classes. Some were free to anyone, others gave heavy discounts to senior citizens, still others required only a commitment to serve for a short time as a volunteer.

When various leaflets and catalogs I had requested began to arrive, I saw that some had been coming all along, addressed simply to "Resident." I had tossed them out as junk mail without reading them, saying to myself, "What possible use could I have for that?!"

I finally selected a class in beginners automobile mechanics! I had a good reason. For thirty-three years I was married to a man who instinctively knew how to fix anything that had moving parts. And both our sons had the same gift. The car's needs were so quickly and effortlessly met that all I ever had to do was to open the door and turn the key. The gas gauge, the oil level, the battery, the tire pressure, to say nothing of more complicated parts and functions, were outside my realm of consciousness.

As a result, when I began to live alone, I was a basket case. My car's behavior simply cowed me. I missed even glaring warnings of trouble. Whenever the poor, neglected mechanism coughed, groaned, shuddered, or jerked, and refused to go, I felt unjustly treated by it. I had no recourse but to have it towed to a repair shop. By then repairs were always long overdue and costly. Anything I could be taught about cars, no matter how minute, would help.

I was the oldest person in the class by several

decades. Thus all my idiocies were in bold relief. I wish I could say that in the end I triumphed magnificently and showed the younger people a thing or two. In fact, I doubtless confirmed their worst old-age stereotypes. I knew scarcely more when the class was over than when it began.

And yet, for me, the class was a resounding success. For the cloud of mystery that had surrounded car behavior was slightly diminished. I was no longer the world's most stupid person in regard to car maintenance. Now I knew almost half as much as the typical driver! And I retained my improved status. Even today, more than a decade later, when my car needs attention, I usually recognize the signs. Since that class, I have not been stranded once beside an immobile automobile, feeling lost at sea in a small boat.

The most important thing I learned from the class is that one need not learn much to gain by studying. A microscopic increase in greatly needed knowledge can make a large difference in one's ability to cope.

Delighted by the results of my mechanics course, I took a survey of philosophy class. I wanted to sharpen my tools for gaining perspective and evaluating experience. As I reviewed in the class the major thought systems of recorded history, I felt the return of my recognition that all ideas are only human interpretations, human conceptions—nothing more. Under the impact of the new theologians, I had sometimes wondered if they were uncovering the real truth.

The most difficult thing in school was the sense of futility some teachers had in teaching me. They found it hard to believe that I could learn or that, if I could, any use would be made of my learning. They kept before me the image of a purposeless little old lady seeking only something to do. My struggle not to internalize that image often took more energy than my studies.

I had to fight against feeling excluded. Many of my fellow students could have been my grandchildren, and my sense of separation from them was heightened in small ways. The roll call would go like this: "Adams, Atkinson, Baldwin, Mrs. Boyle, Brown, Carlton, Jones . . ." By the third day, my name often was omitted. I knew the obvious and innocent reason for the omission. Since I was easily recognized by the teacher, my name could be checked on the list without being called. But when names all around me were reiterated day after day and mine was skipped, I simply felt erased. However, this experience was before the notion of continuing education for senior citizens had taken hold. In classes and workshops today, I'm much less likely to be the only old person there.

In a Survey of Western Culture class, the professor—whom I will call Dr. Purdue—was a dynamic, well-informed man in his forties. At our first session, he stressed the importance of not categorizing persons or groups. "I allow myself a prejudice against only one group of people," he said, "*Prejudiced* people." I thought, "At last! A class that will be a haven!"

During our second session, he caught himself in the middle of a sentence, grinned engagingly and said, "But I told you that story last time. I must be eighty years old." The students laughed, attracted by his freedom to laugh at himself.

Later, Dr. Purdue again stressed the stupidity of stereotyping. He told a story about the famous black columnist and commentator, Carl Rowan. According to the story, Rowan was mowing his lawn one day when a white couple on his block—"probably elderly," Dr. Purdue interpolated—asked what he charged "for doing lawns." (According to the full story, which Dr. Purdue, for some reason did not tell, Rowan replied, "Well, that all depends. One nice white lady sleeps with me for it.")

Later, in emphasizing how ridiculous people appear when they close their minds to changing times, Dr. Purdue recounted a recent experience in the Museum of Modern Art. As he stood admiring an internationally famous abstract painting, he heard "two old codgers discussing it. 'Kids in kindergarten do better than that,' one said, and the other cackled and agreed."

I am a slow learner. I still wasn't prepared for his closing remark at our next session. After a haggling discussion with class members over a certain theory of cultural change, he shrugged and said, "Oh, well. All this hot air isn't accomplishing anything. We've been carrying on like a bunch of old women!"

I continued in the class as a personal discipline and with the hope of helping Dr. Purdue see his unconscious stereotyping. An opportunity finally came to point out privately that "in this one area, you sometimes slip into implications I'm sure you don't intend." He truculently replied that he was only telling good stories. "Don't let the years bury your sense of humor," he advised.

Like all of us, Dr. Purdue had a blind spot. He never would have allowed a student to get away with similar implications in regard to any other minority group. But his own bias against the old seemed to him to be pure realism. He wouldn't have dreamed of telling stories about Jews, or of saying that we had all been shooting off hot air like a bunch of blacks.

"Suppose," I said to him, "that every day I told a story or made a remark in which the humor always hung on some professorial weakness. Wouldn't you eventually get the message that I didn't think highly of professors?"

He deflected my point with a twist of his mental wrist. "You've put your finger right on your problem," he said. "You've got it in for professors."

I shouldn't have been surprised at his resistance. Few of us can handle even a hint that we fall short in what we think is our greatest strength.

Another odd example of stereotyping appeared when I registered for another class. After checking my forms, the assistant registrar said casually, "These are OK. Sign here and here, Mother."

Startled, I gave him a searching look. He was chubby, bald and barely ten years my junior. Even with a pre-teen pregnancy, I couldn't quite have managed him. I wanted to reply, "OK, sonny boy!" I regretted having suppressed that reply when he patted my hand and murmured, "Going to school does keep the mind young, doesn't it, Mother?"

I must add that some school officials and teachers were wonderful and made me feel accepted, an asset, and personally full of potential. As my faith seeped back, I began to see persons who possessed that touch as instruments of God. One by one, they restored my sense of being watched over, loved, and directed by him. Their appearance when my personhood most needed confirming seemed too regular to be coincidence.

I took at least one class, sometimes as many as three, each term. There were some negative moments, but I always netted a few gains. In a home economics class, I learned to use a sewing machine. It was clear from the start that I would never be a tailor, but I gained many small freedoms in mending and altering. In a beauty school, I took a class in hair dressing and learned to give myself permanents, shampoos, and sets. I will never win a prize as a hair dresser, but I did win my independence from beauty shops. And the money saved has more than paid for all my other classes.

In a class on investment, I learned the difference between stocks and bonds, a distinction that once had seemed the merest technicality. As an extra dividend, I acquired enough of the strange language of finance to listen with interest to conversations about the stock market. *That* is progress!

From classes in psychology, I gained new insights in understanding people. From lay school classes at a theological seminary, I painfully worked toward a more confident understanding of my faith. And in a class on creative writing, I received an object lesson that increased my understanding of the five darkening years that had just passed.

I took the course to become a more objective critic of my own writing. But of greater value was what I learned from noting my feelings when, in a class of thirty-seven young people, I made the best grade in the course. That shouldn't have surprised me. I had written three books and several hundred articles, and after all, this was a junior college class. But I reacted with incredulous ecstasy. I felt as if I had won the Nobel prize for literature. Only then did I fully grasp the depth to which old-age stereotypes had undercut even my common sense.

14

"Let Justice
Roll Down"

I was well launched into the adventure of recouping my losses when I received a summons to serve for a month on jury duty. I was both repelled and intrigued. Jury duty, I was told, is exhausting, dull, and painful. Further, my observations during the civil rights struggle in the South had convinced me that justice is not always accomplished in court.

On the other hand, I had never served on a jury. An important part of the adventure of recovery surely must be trying new things. I was informed that I could be excused for reasons of age or health. I decided to serve. It proved to be one of the most important learning experiences of my life.

On the first day, I learned that in civil cases thirteen names would be drawn but only seven jurors would be used. Each lawyer must eliminate three, without stating reasons. If he or she had objections to none, he would strike out three names at random. (In criminal cases, when felony was involved, twenty names would be drawn and twelve jurors used.) So in the several cases where my name was stricken, I didn't know whether I was deemed unsuitable or was only eliminated at random. Though I was curious as to why I was eliminated, I thought the practice sound.

The first time my name was called, one of the lawyers eliminated me. The second time, I was astonished to have to eliminate myself. I had always thought myself uncommonly objective and had imagined I could be fair to anyone. But when I learned that the defendant was accused of bullying and harassment, and that he was a member of the National Socialist White People's Party (American Nazis), I instantly felt he was more likely to be guilty than an ordinary person, and I knew I couldn't be trusted to judge him solely on the evidence. When I disqualified myself, three other persons followed suit. I later learned he had been convicted. To my horror, I was glad! The judge had commended us for disqualifying ourselves. Now I saw why. I had repressed a temptation to stay on the jury and nail the so-and-so while I had the chance!

Later, I disqualified myself again—in more embarrassing circumstances. A young couple was accused of cheating another couple in a real estate deal. I failed to realize my bias at the time the judge asked us to confess biases. But the more I looked at the defendants, the more they looked like typical crooks. The impression became so strong that without having heard any evidence whatever I was almost sure they were guilty. I had to interrupt the proceedings:

"Your Honor, I find I have feelings that make me fear I might not be objective in this case. May I step down?"

Foolishly, I hoped he would take my word for it. But he said, "I think the court and the attorneys would like to hear your reasons."

I thought I would die. What could I say?

"It sounds so silly, I feel like a fool," I floundered. "But the defendants' faces remind me of persons I have good reason to distrust. It might influence my judgment."

He said, "That's very candid of you. You may step down." And as I left the jury box, the attorney for the defense came over and thanked me.

The next day, I was chosen for a jury of seven. I was the only woman. The plaintiff was a twenty-three-year-old girl whose car, two and a half years before, had been hit broadside by a man who ran a red light. Since then she had suffered severe pains in her head, neck, and back, and had spent over $5,000 in medical bills. She was suing the man for $50,000.

I had long been bored and irritated by endless streams of suits, often brought without good reason. Thus, I felt some sympathy for the accused. But after the evidence was in, I was convinced the girl was telling the truth.

The trial dragged on hour after hour. Both lawyers beat every dead horse to a pulp. When the testimony was concluded and the summaries were made, it was past three o'clock on the second day of the trial. Filing out to the jury room, we were bored and very tired. But I was soon roused by a series of shocks.

First, I learned that three of the six other jurors seemed to resent any woman trying to get any money from any man for any reason. One of them shamelessly felt that the only really pertinent fact in the case was not introduced in testimony—that suits like this raise insurance rates for us all. He held out, against witnesses and other strong evidence, that the accused had the green light. On the first vote, we split four to three as to who was responsible for the accident. But when we read the judge's instructions, and reviewed the evidence, the three dissenters conceded that the man was at fault.

It troubled me that only two of the seven of us had observed the many clues indicating that the man was lying and the girl telling a straight story. Troubling also was the fact that the juror who worried about insurance rates was the last to concede that the accused was guilty.

We moved on to the amount of the settlement. All agreed that $50,000 was too much, our only point of agreement without debate during the entire case. The girl was suffering but not incapacitated. Doctors agreed that with medication she could function up to 90 percent of her capacity and might continue to improve.

I thought $25,000 appropriate. The three hostile men thought only her local medical bills should be paid. They objected to reimbursing her even for out-of-town specialists. The other three men recommended, consecutively, $8,000, $15,000, and $10,-000. After lengthy discussion, one of the three hostile men broke ranks.

"Since we're four to three in favor of giving her more, I'll agree to full reimbursement of all medical costs, in town and out, plus her out-of-pocket losses for time lost from work—altogether $6,500."

The other two die-hards said they would go with paying all medical expenses, but no refunds for lost wages. Whereupon my sole semi-ally said he would be willing to come down to $13,500.

Seeing how things were going, I decided to take my stand where I had at least some support. I said, "I think she deserves $25,000, but I'll settle for $15,000 if all will agree."

It was now nine o'clock. We had spent most of the

day in court and over five hours in the jury room. With a let's-go-home glint in their eyes, the two hardest die-hards said that to get unanimous agreement they would come up to $6,500. That way, they said, the girl would lose nothing by the accident, but neither would she make money on it.

"Not so," I said. "She would lose future medical expenses and any damage to her career resulting from inability to function at full capacity, and money deducted in future for extra sick leave because of head and back pain."

The die-hard who first broke ranks by suggesting $6,500 said that was true, and he would be willing to come up to $8,000. The semi-ally who had named $10,000 as fair said that considering the lateness of the hour, he would come down to $8,000. The man who had originally named $15,000 said he thought he could live with $8,000, though he thought she deserved more. They all turned expectant eyes on me. I said nothing.

Silence fell in the jury room. After a while, the foreman reread aloud the judge's instructions. There was another silence. Then one of the two men still holding out for $6,500 said, "In view of the judge's guidelines and the fact that it's after ten o'clock, even though I don't think she deserves $8,000, I'll go along if everyone else will."

That left only myself and the die-hard who didn't want to raise insurance rates. He said firmly, "I couldn't live with myself for days if I gave that girl more than her bare expenses."

Another long silence. It was broken by one of my semi-allies rereading the part of the judge's instructions about awarding the plaintiff "compensation for physical suffering and mental anguish, as well as reimbursement for costs and losses, should you find in her favor." Then the hardest die-hard said, "Well, I guess I'll just have to stand a bad conscience for a few days. It's ten thirty. I'll allow the $8,000. Let's go home." All eyes turned on me.

I could see, feel, and hear the tension rising. It was like an old-fashioned soap opera. The six male jurors were getting angrier by the minute. I felt like a little old lady in tennis shoes saying in effect, "God help me, I can do no other!"

But I was shocked by the emphasis on the lateness of the hour. We weren't there to get home early or to keep insurance costs down. We were there to see that justice was done.

I said, "I hate to do this to you all, and I know you're awfully mad with me. But you must remember that I'm down from $25,000. If this girl is telling the truth—and I believe she is—$15,000 is a pittance for what she's had to endure through no fault of her own. I couldn't live with myself, not just for a few days but for the rest of my life, if I came any lower just because six handsome, charming, intelligent, vigorous men put pressure on me to do it."

They all laughed, and the tension was relieved a mite.

My semi-allies suggested $10,000, then $12,000, then $13,500. I began to feel more and more like a stubborn fool. But I knew I wasn't. What I had said was true and still valid. The $13,500 would still be $1,500 out of that poor girl's pocket, just because I wasn't willing to feel like a stubborn fool. And I said so.

I went to the ladies room in preparation for an extended sit-down strike. I stayed longer than necessary, to let the men discuss the situation without me. When I came out, the dark looks had lightened. One of my semi-allies said, "Did we agree on $14,000?" I said, "My figure was $15,000." And they said almost pleasantly, "OK. $15,000 it is."

I thanked them and said I was sorry I had held them up so long. My strongest semi-ally said he was glad, because his daughter had suffered a similar injury ten years ago, and she still suffered bad headaches from it. Two of the three die-hards said they had conceded because "the contest was too uneven." They meant that gallant men could not bring themselves to beat a frail, lone, little old lady into submission through sheer exhaustion.

I smiled sweetly and thanked them for their chivalry. I kept my secret that I felt bright-eyed and bushy-tailed and had been quite willing and able to remain in the jury room for as many days as necessary to get that poor girl her $15,000.

In fact, I was astonished at my rediscovery of a truth I had almost forgotten since my long ago contests in the battle-torn South: that when there is nothing personally to gain from making a stand other than that it is right, strength is gained from the very substance of God's creation. And weariness is minimized.

My tour of jury duty left me with new respect for our legal system. With the many kinds of human weaknesses and faults we all have, it was heartening to note how fully they were foreseen by the creators of our system, and how protections were added for individual justice. The cross-examination of witnesses, while often dull or harsh, is effective in uncovering hidden facts. The judge's instructions enlightened, strengthened, and guided us beyond our natural capacities. And after all, I was only a little old lady in tennis shoes who never had served on a jury before; yet our system permitted me to function unhandicapped. Our system allowed a small person with a big conviction to triumph over powerful opponents who were less sure of the nature of their task and of the direction in which they should go. In the jury room, it doesn't matter that we have a youth-oriented culture and a tradition of male rule.

As I ended my month of service, I felt happy about our nation. More than in many years, I felt America deserved to endure. I was filled with good feelings about my country and the blueprint of her charter. I experienced again the tingling of belonging and of conscious citizenship. And I knew I would be a better, stronger citizen for having served.

Moreover, I felt happy about myself. The experience pushed me far upward on my climb to inner health. My personhood had triumphed over age and stereotypes! Once more, I tasted the exhilarating wine of feeling fully human.

"Behold, I Am Doing a New Thing"

At times I felt my old self. Accepting what I could not change brought large areas of peace and renewed energy. Changing what I could was more fun than expected. And more reassuring. It gave me some control over my situation. I loved reclaiming a sense of progress and autonomy. Even though my new skills and understandings were small, their message was large. I could improve!

But other sore areas remained. One was a smoldering fear of the future. I felt I was only negotiating a reprieve. Eventually, the erosion of time would make all those hateful stereotypes of inadequacy real. My reconstructed sense of progress could not indefinitely withstand the assault of years.

I shuddered away from the thought. But the drip, drip, drip of our youth culture's messages would not let me forget. In spite of myself, I wondered if the stereotypes did not already apply, or would apply sooner than I thought. I saw no way to reduce that fear. At times it engulfed me.

I attended any discussion groups that sounded promising, especially when they focused on personal problems. In a group of physically handicapped persons gathered to hear a special speaker, I got the longed-for clue.

The speaker's face was tranquil as he sat in a wheelchair. His name was Sam. His first words hooked me.

"No matter how scary your losses and prospects are, there's a way to be a whole person."

The expression of his face and the timbre of his voice reinforced his words. They made me believe he would not offer easy formulas but would tell us how he had climbed from his own despair. I reached for my notebook and pencil.

"When I woke in the hospital after the plane crash and saw I was this way," he pointed to his useless legs, "I just stared at a corner of the ceiling for days, maybe weeks. Longing for the past and dread of the future tormented me. When I graduated to a wheelchair, I didn't feel much better. I saw that chair as a steel trap.

"When an old friend came to see me, the first thing I said was, 'Charlie, I can't face all those months and years out there waiting—crouching!'

"He took my hand and I felt the warmth and energy that was running through him. 'Listen, Sam,' he told me. 'You don't have to face all those months and years. *All you have to face is the next couple of minutes.*' "

Sam paused. I began to tingle in that special way we sometimes do when a message comes that is clearly for us.

"When Charlie explained, I got my first clue to living with things that are too hard to live with. You do it by focusing on what's happening right now. Not on what's already happened. Not on what's going to happen. But on this very minute. You may think this little minute empty. It isn't. Not if you're fully into it.

When you're totally in it, your eyes and ears open up.

"Folks, believe me. You can handle any problem when you take it one minute at a time. The greatest prophet in the Old Testament knew that and said don't worry about yesterday. Jesus knew it and said don't worry about tomorrow."

Sam told us that at first, living only in the present had sounded unreal. But what Charlie said stayed with him. And one thing was clear: there was nothing to lose but despair. As he persisted, he saw that the worst thing about living in a wheelchair was the thought of never doing anything else—looking back and thinking, "But that's all over now!"; looking forward and thinking, "How can I stand it?" Suddenly he realized that his life wasn't as changed as he had thought.

"I didn't ever walk much, and I didn't much enjoy what little walking I did," Sam confessed. "I drove to work, sat at a desk all day, and—wouldn't you know?—first thing when I got home I headed for my armchair! Weekends, I liked to lie around reading, listening to music, watching TV, and sitting in the yard beating my gums with friends. I doubt if I spent more than one hour a day doing things I can't do now. I'd taken it for granted my life was ruined. I even prided myself on 'facing the truth' squarely. Could the real steel trap be not my wheelchair but my mourning the past and dreading the future? Maybe nothing but me kept me from enjoying most of the things I had always enjoyed. Then I got a surprise."

Sam looked from one face to another. His expression reflected the excitement he felt over what he was about to share. "You aren't going to believe this, folks. But in some ways I enjoy life more! When I stick with right now, I see and hear things I never knew were there.

"It wasn't the long ago past or the far ahead future that had me trapped. What trapped me were the things that had just happened, or were just about to happen. I was so hung up on yesterday and tomorrow that I completely missed the wonderful things going on right then. I didn't even know when the shrubbery began to bud! Is that a little true for you, too? Don't you sometimes wake up in September and wonder where the spring and summer went?"

With a shock, I saw that I did. My consciousness regularly skipped the present. The heaviest burdens I carried were the future and the past.

"The trouble with that kind of living," Sam went on, "is that it's just not real! The real world is one instant in time—*right now*. When we live in right now, there's no such thing as a boring or anxious day. The real world is fascinating. We make all our experiences gray by looking only ahead or behind. People who are dying sometimes tell me they've just discovered the present moment. Just when life is going away, they're learning how to live. I hope you won't wait till then."

Sam's message sank deep. Centuries before Christ, Isaiah thundered in the name of God, "Remember not . . . the things of old! . . . Behold, I am doing a new thing" (Isa. 43:18-19). Later St. Paul affirmed, "One thing I do: forgetting what lies behind . . . , I press on" (Phil. 3:13-14). Jesus himself told us to deal with today, and that tomorrow would deal with itself.

Again and again, the Bible points to the eternal now. Yet I had been plodding on, dragging yesterday after me and staggering under the weight of tomorrow. Incidents that hurt, angered or frightened me drew much of their dark power from associations with memories or anticipations. Painful experiences just encountered, injustices just endured, mistakes just made, opportunities just lost, and failures just scored pushed crucial current issues from my mind. Probably not more than 2 or 3 percent of my thoughts focused sharply on present reality. And inadequacy, failure, and defeat were the heavy interest I paid on my borrowed trouble.

Now, I realized that only the present can be acted in. Problems of the past and future can only be reviewed, worried over, circled round and round. Good memories can be refreshing, and bad ones can be learned from. But, good or bad, when memories hamper present functioning, it is time to turn them out. There is a place for pondering the future, when present actions or decisions can alter its outcome. But when tomorrow appears only as an instrument of destruction, anxiety alone results.

Focusing on the present is not an easy discipline. But as awareness of the eternal now worked its magic in my consciousness, the world around me began to sparkle and shine. I perceived sunlight in a different way. Flowers, trees, clouds, the richly varied music of nature and of man rounded out and became full. Friends appeared more vibrant, pristine, alive. I was more aware of myself. Longing, timidity, hope, appreciation, anger, joy, and gratitude moved visibly inside me. A new dimension expanded my consciousness of stars, moon, warmth of fire, and bracing sting of wind. Nature's abundance and variety burst upon me with a shock. In my marrow and muscle, I felt the sometimes hastening, sometimes plodding energy of all living things.

Above all, I felt the overwhelming majesty of God and my own dependence on him. The world of the present is the one that God makes. Our images of our yesterdays and tomorrows are our own handiwork. We choose to live in the dull, dim, aching, unreal worlds we make, instead of in Eden. By that choice we bring upon us exile.

What
Gerontologists Say

Focusing on the present is important for free
and vital living at any time. It is essential when one is overwhelmed. And in our culture,
the old are overwhelmed.

Dr. Robert N. Butler and Myrna L. Lewis in their
book *Aging and Mental Health,* (St. Louis: Mosby,
1977), summarize the typical situation of the old (the
italics are mine).

Losses in every aspect of late life compel the elderly to
expend enormous amounts of physical and emotional
energy in . . . adapting to changes . . . : *death* of the marital
partner, older friends, colleagues, relatives; *decline* of
physical health and coming to personal terms with death;
loss of status, prestige, and participation in society; . . .
burdens of marginal living standards . . . *cultural devaluation*
and *neglect.* . . . In addition, *new modes of adaptation* become
necessary. . . . Notice is seldom taken of the amount of *new
learning* an old person must undergo to adapt to the
accelerating changes in body, feelings and environment. As
with any new learning, *anxiety* develops in proportion to
the task. . . . Frequently anxiety and its expressions are
incorrectly diagnosed as "senility" and *wrongly considered*

untreatable. (Until recently Dr. Butler was Director of the National Institute on Aging. He is now Chairman of the Department of Geriatrics and Adult Development at the Mt. Sinai School of Medicine in New York. Ms. Lewis is a mental health specialist.)

Reading the Butler-Lewis book gave me such feelings of being understood and returned to the human race that I had to learn more about current research on aging. I discovered vast amounts, and the findings were exciting.

Especially restorative was the Baltimore Longitudinal Study, which was conducted at the Gerontology Research Center of the National Institute on Aging. This long and thorough project was launched in 1958 and is still in progress. Six hundred and fifty healthy volunteers, some old, some young, were selected. Each was questioned, examined, and tested exhaustively for two and a half days. A detailed physical, mental, emotional, and social profile of each person was drawn. Every one to two years thereafter, the same battery of examinations and tests were repeated. Thus, researchers were able to compare members of the elderly group, whose ages ranged from sixty-five to ninety-one, with members of the youthful group, where the average age was twenty-one. The comparisons also enabled the researchers to pinpoint changes that resulted from aging.

To the surprise of most of the researchers, the minds of the healthy elderly continued to function normally as they grew older. In some respects they even improved. Indeed, the old in several ways performed better than the young.

General slowing down was found to be typical in aging. But when the old were allowed to work at their own speed, new skills, new knowledge, new ideas, and new points of view were easily acquired. The healthy old were characteristically, in Dr. Butler's words, "flexible, resourceful, and optimistic."

At the same time, Jack W. Taylor, director of executive development at Planning Dynamics in Pittsburgh, instituted a project that illustrated the above findings. In a series of creativity training programs throughout the United States, Taylor tested participants before and after their training. Later, follow-up tests measured how well the training was applied on the job. During a twenty-some year period, persons over forty improved during training more than twice as much as those under thirty. Further, roughly 80 percent of all the most workable ideas came from those over forty. For further details of Taylor's work, see *Don't Give Up on an Aging Parent,* by Lawrence Galton (New York: Crown Publishers, 1975).

Taylor is just one of a growing number of researchers who have found that older workers often more than make up for their deliberate pace by being more efficient. They commonly work more steadily with fewer absences, make wiser decisions concerning where to focus efforts, make fewer mistakes, and take more pride in a job well done than young workers. Upon observation, some of the touted speed of inexperienced workers proves simply to result from unawareness of possible errors and problems.

Today when competence is seen as on the skids by age forty, such findings are crucial. But it's worth noting that two generations ago, they would have been thought self-evident and trite. Only recently has it not been taken for granted that performance improves with age and experience.

Our uniquely modern problem of seeing old people as obsolete stems from several factors. One is that with our small, nuclear families and over-busy lives, people tend to grow up with no close contact with any old persons. And in dealing with unfamiliar groups, it is the striking and especially shocking behavior, rather than expected and normal behavior, that sticks in our minds. Thus, stereotypes are formed from those rare but memorable examples. The more bizarre the deviation, the more firmly fixed are the stereotypes. In societies (such as ours of a century ago) where all ages live together with coordinated responsibilities, the real abilities of the old are recognized. And their individual weaknesses are realistically taken in stride.

Another factor is our emphasis on speed and productivity. *Hurry!* is almost our national motto. Conscientiously careful workers are out of style. Since slowing down is a normal part of aging, the old are at a real disadvantage when demands are made for ever greater speed. People of all ages when under pressure to perform more quickly than they actually can, will lose confidence, psychologically block, make mistakes, and become confused. *These are symptoms of pressure, not of incompetence.* But in the old they are interpreted as signs of deteriorating faculties. And a vicious circle of tension and increased symptoms begins.

The greatest single factor in creating negative stereotypes of the elderly, however, may have come from the first fumbling efforts of old age research itself. Between 1920 and 1955, almost all research on aging was done on people in hospitals, nursing homes, mental institutions, and the like. Offering the grimmest possible picture of old age, these severely incapacitated people comprised less than 5 percent of the elderly population. But because they were easily accessible, almost all the data on aging was gained from those unrepresentative few. That data was printed in reports, then passed along to the public through the media.

Now, the tide of ageism has begun to turn. A group of highly trained scientists met in 1955 and resolved to get a more realistic picture of human aging by studying, not the helpless 5 percent, but the many healthy old people who remained active. A nation-wide series of studies began, aimed at discerning which common symptoms in old age resulted from aging itself and which from disease, malnutrition, general neglect of body and mind, lack of stimulation, lack of social interaction, and from depression, grief, and despair.

The notion that persons steadily lose competence through the years runs counter to common sense, to the large contributions to humanity made by many persons over seventy, and to beliefs held by most people in most times and cultures since the beginning of history. Now, such a notion also runs counter to the findings of modern research.

However, old age is so firmly linked to mental decay in most minds that old people who are undeniably sharp are regarded as freaks, like four-year-olds who can play Beethoven and Bach. Despite the mounting number of gerontologists who loudly protest the connection, the linking clanks on. Stereotypes wear like iron.

Dr. Alex Comfort is one who protests. Dr. Comfort is a physician, medical biologist, gerontologist, author, and lecturer in the Department of Psychiatry at Stanford University.

"The human brain does not shrink, wilt, perish, or deteriorate with age," he writes in *A Good Age* (New York: Simon & Schuster, 1976). "It normally continues to function well through as many as nine decades. . . . Dementia in old age is neither general nor common, but because it piles up in hospitals, it is visible and frightening."

Less than one percent of people over seventy can expect to suffer from senile dementia, Dr. Comfort asserts. "Loss of brain cells, often put at some figure like 100,000 per day, probably reflects not age damage but some programmed clear-out process. The figure is trifling anyhow, and massive loss is always due to disease. Now that brain damage is no longer considered a right and proper part of aging, some of these diseases . . . may be preventable."

Welcome assurance! Talk of losing up to one hundred thousand brain cells a day terrified me, as it does most lay people. We are told that lost brain cells are never replaced and that almost half are gone forever by age eighty. This sounds as if eighty-year-olds are only half as intelligent as young people. Few of us know that we have such an oversupply of brain cells—something like thirteen billion—that as with fish eggs, acorns, and many other natural resources, brain cells greatly exceed the number needed for their specific function. We could lose well over half and still have billions more than we would ever need.

Gerontologist Dr. David Stonecypher says in his book, *Getting Older and Staying Younger,* that much deterioration in aging comes from the fact that "we abandon the older person to 'rust.' " Compulsory retirement makes old people feel so useless that they stop trying. Then they rust. In his words, "Those functions—physical, and mental—which are exercised tend to persist: those which are not exercised tend to disappear."

Dr. Lissy Jarvik, after many years of studying intellectual functioning in an aging population, states that decline in knowledge and reasoning ability seldom occurs until nearly a score of years past the usual retirement age. She is a professor of psychiatry at the University of California at Los Angeles, and is a member of the advisory board for the Center For Aging at Wadsworth Veterans Administration Hospital. Much that we assume is deteriorated memory, she adds, results from other causes, such as heavy stress or depression. These distresses can reduce interest and affect the person's ability to concentrate. A good memory is often restored, she points out, simply through counseling or anti-depressant drugs.

Authorities on aging now say that mental deterioration in the old often stems from the kinds of things that cause deterioration at any age. Dr. Tom Leo Smith, a University of Denver social psychologist, says he produced forgetfulness, living in the past, and general signs of senility in young people in their twenties and thirties, who volunteered for the experiment. These symptoms began only hours after the volunteers were consistently ignored, had their opinions discounted, and were made to feel they had no useful function in society.

Given the kind of verbal and nonverbal messages old people continually receive, anyone will begin to lose effectiveness. Once people are convinced they are substandard, and especially if they expect only to become more so, they cannot compete with those who have the stimulation of self-confidence and the reinforcement of confidence from others.

A negative stereotype places so many handicaps on

its objects that it is almost impossible for them to function at full capacity. In the early 1900s, any suggestion that females of any race or blacks of either sex could compete intellectually on equal terms with white males was thought ridiculous even by most women and most blacks. The result in both groups was that their members so lacked confidence in themselves that they often endorsed the stereotypes and acted them out. Old people, too, absorb the destructive images that are pressed upon them, and by autohypnosis make them true.

"The Log in My Own Eye"

With my discoveries confirmed by scientific research, I began to feel again that I was an insider in my world. And I didn't want anyone to be an outsider. All around me old people were suffering as I had suffered, not knowing how to lessen their pain. An urge to give them solutions pushed up in me like a growing tree.

Among my acquaintances was a charming woman who had recently retired and was living alone. Characteristically active and practical, Sadie now flung herself into community work. She obviously enjoyed bringing her abundant common sense and many skills to her new tasks. But when deteriorating vision forced her to stop driving, she dropped all her activities and stayed home.

"Why not use taxis?" I asked, knowing she could afford them.

A look of desperation crossed her face. "Because I've always driven myself. All my life I've been free as a bird. Now that's all over."

"But it needn't be!" I cried, with the crusading zeal of a recent convert. "Forget what you used to do. Just start with what you can do right now. You'll find lots of new ways to do the things you like best. Using taxis will soon be as easy as your own car."

"Oh, I think cab companies are robbers," she said.

I spent an hour pointing out the headaches and costs of keeping a car—installment payments, garage, insurance, state and local registration, parking fees, gas, general maintenance, and major repairs. When the total was divided by the number of times Sadie had driven her car in a typical week, it was clear that using taxis actually would save her money. I looked up from my labors with a sense of accomplishment. There was no answering look of relief on Sadie's face.

"I never had to use taxis," she repeated sharply. "I always just got in my car and went."

My bewilderment was generously laced with repressed righteous wrath. Why was she angry? *I* was the one who had slaved away fruitlessly, trying to help!

But after a few months of helping various other people in ways that I, not they, elected, I realized I was doing to Sadie and the others precisely what I had found so destructive when done to me! Ignoring their own strengths and resources, I had insisted on personally meeting their needs—or what I thought were their needs. And the unintended message of my stance was that they couldn't handle problems that were quite, quite easy for me! After making them feel they were impotent receivers of my bountiful gifts, I was outraged that they weren't pleased! It amounted to exploitation. I wanted them to make me feel good by accepting my solutions and being happy with them ever after.

I was totally humbled and totally confused. The troubled persons I had reached out to needed some kind of help. I certainly had needed it—and had felt very lonely when my groping hand wasn't grasped. Sadie had needed it, too. Her uncharacteristic harping on her losses was a clear cry for help. Yet in hastily grabbing hands, I had often done more harm than good—like the people who rush to help accident victims and try to move them without knowing where their injuries are!

A tiny light flashed in my foggy depths. So that was what I had been doing! I had plunged into being helpful without bothering to notice whether my help was needed or desired. I had been so busy cloning my solutions for others that I hadn't focused on their personhood!

Horrified, I reassessed the situation. A message hurtled down to me straight from Matthew 7:3, 5. "Why do you see the speck that is in your brother's eye, but do not notice the log that is in your own eye? . . . You hypocrite, first take the log out of your own eye, and then you will see clearly to take the speck out of your brother's eye." My condemnation of those who had dehumanized me had boomeranged.

Needed, desired help is beautiful and healing. It draws people close. Indeed, I think it is God's own delegated love. But unneeded, undesired help tells its victims plainly that they are not being cared about but used. Sadie did not want my solutions. She was very able to develop her own. Pushing mine on her implied that she could not cope with her challenges—thus adding insult to the injury her failing eyes had already dealt.

There were several clues to her real needs, had I looked for them. One was her character. She was independent, strong, brave. She considered herself a problem solver, and she was proud of her coping skills. Another was that in her new plight, she had reacted in ways not typical of her. That meant the threat was overwhelming. A third was her anger at the kind of help I offered. As I put these clues together, I saw that her chief need was for reassurance—reassurance that no handicap could keep her from being who she was. My insistence that she use my solutions must have seemed a dreadful confirmation that others would now seize her baton and try to direct her life.

If I had confirmed her very real resourcefulness and strength instead of her fears, that would have helped. If I had tried to show her that because of who she was, she would be always essentially autonomous and free, respected, admired, and loved, that would have helped. If I had reminded her that her problem-solving skills had blessed her and others all her life and would not fail her now, that would have helped. In short, stressing her built-in resources and personal worth, would have eased the hard task of marshaling her courage, confidence and skill against the threat of helplessness.

What Sadie needed and wanted from me was a listening ear, an interested mind, a caring heart, and a willingness to let her be herself. Aren't these the offerings most of us need and want from our family and friends? Isn't that the kind of help God gives us? And aren't we supposed to pass it on?

It was now nearly two years since I had begun my slow climb back to well-being. By using my guide-lines—accept, change, live in the eternal now—I had regained much of my old confidence and zest. But after my poor performance with Sadie and others, I saw a great remaining gap in my wholeness. Giving is essential to being fully human. We must contribute to be fulfilled. If I could not give others what I had gained, meaning would be absent from both my pain and my recovery.

I decided to learn to discern the real needs of others and how to fill them. Why not offer myself as a general volunteer to my church, to retirement homes, and to nursing homes? Then I would see what kinds of help people asked of me.

Quickly, I discovered that most people want help in only one or two areas, regardless of how many needs they have. A former opera singer in her eighties wanted me to take her once a week for a dutch treat lunch and a little shopping. She enjoyed every part of these outings—the drive, the food, the conversation, the shops. She looked forward to them week after week. But she would accept no other services. She treasured her independence more than other satis-factions and would surrender it only at one point.

A blind woman named Estelle wanted me to read to her, to write an endless stream of letters for her, and to stand by as she toiled in her garden. But beyond my eyesight she wanted nothing. She dictated, folded, stamped, and mailed all letters herself. In the garden, she did all digging, planting, weeding, fertilizing, and watering. She told me to put the hose in her hand and to turn it off and on when she said to. Other than that I could only stand and watch. Rarely did she ask me to identify a plant. She preferred to do it herself by touch. She nettled at unsolicited help, even if she was about to make a mistake. I noted with embarrassment that her behavior made me feel totally useless. To feel helpful, I needed to run the show!

I devoted three hours every Tuesday and Friday to these passive services. Estelle made it clear she wanted more. But although I admired and respected her enormously, I felt unable to endure more of that level of passivity. However, I was glad to give her extra time by including her in some of my activities. I would telephone and ask her to join me in my walk through my oasis where she could hear water gurgle and birds sing. Or I would invite her to come with me to a civic or a religious meeting or to a class I thought she might like.

She always accepted with manifest delight. But when I arrived, dressed for the occasion and eager for the physical or mental exercise in store, she unfailingly guided me with an iron hand either to the desk to write "some extra urgent letters" or to the garden for some botanical emergency that didn't exist. There I would sit, pining for my walk or my meeting, while I acquired writer's cramp and a numb gluteus maximus muscle. Or I would stand idle while she vigorously dug, weeded, and watered a garden that needed no attention.

Eventually I learned that her chosen tasks were the only ones she intended to do with me. For a walk, she preferred a familiar route which she followed without help. For mental stimulation, she liked to turn on her radio or talking books, with no help from anyone.

There were persons who wanted transportation only—to the doctor, the dentist, the store. There were those who wanted a friendly visit only and delighted in serving me refreshments. I was appalled to find that even though I knew the chance to be a gracious hostess is a real need, I still felt discomforted at their efforts on my behalf. One woman wished me just to sit with her, doing nothing, saying nothing. She said to bring a book and read—to myself, not her! She liked company but wanted neither talk nor action.

Another woman wanted me for just two things: to take her to dress shops, and to pray with her. She said she never wearied of trying on dresses and that she felt cut off from the love of God when there wasn't plenty of vocalized prayer.

The one consistent message I got from all these varied persons was that maintaining the independence they still had was paramount. The aspect of my services they valued most was that I did what they chose to have me do. They were aching for a sense of some control over their lives. This agonized need for independence isn't so much a characteristic of the old as of handicapped people at any age. I once saw a bedridden young woman burst into tears because a nursing home attendant insisted on cutting her toenails on a day she hadn't chosen.

"They never let me decide anything for myself," she sobbed.

I understood and said so. Decision making is an essential part of being human. When it is threatened, it becomes more valuable to the person than his or her bodily well-being. One can be fully human without good health or physical strength. One cannot be fully human without freedom to choose.

"But They Hear Not"

Thanks to my three guidelines—accept what you can't change, change what you can, and focus on the eternal now—many of my needs were being met. I felt more tranquil than ever before. Yet deep inside me, a lonely vacuum still waited . . . waited.

I performed endless small services for many people. But the warm exchange of human closeness was missing. I lacked true interlocking with other lives. No one sought me for things of first importance. Yet I was sure I had been more nourished than weakened by the years. Somewhere in the great, heaving ocean of human need, wasn't there some essential, longed-for service I could perform?

Warm memories began to rise. Throughout my life special people had briefly sustained me when no one else had. When I was a small child, an adolescent, a young adult, a middle-aged woman, an old woman— those special people dissolved my loneliness, enabled me to take heart, discover myself, believe in my future, find solutions, and feel at home in my world. I wanted to do for others what those people had done for me.

How had they achieved their miracles of healing?

There seemed little common ground among them. They were a variety of ages from very young to very old. They were of both sexes, many professions, many points of view. I hadn't thought of them as helpers, only as friends. What made them different from other friends who hadn't helped at all?

Well, they never seemed preoccupied or in a hurry when we were together. They gave me their full attention when we talked. They listened, really listened, joining me in my sorrows and joys, no matter how trivial those sorrows and joys were. They seemed truly interested in me—everything about me. They took me seriously. They enjoyed me! And they were honest with me about what they thought and felt. By these simple means, they delivered the message that I was of value. And by that message, I was confirmed in who I was and what I wanted to be.

Could I learn to deliver that message? It seemed a vocation tailor-made for the old. Why? Because we have finished more of our lives and therefore are not as pressured by ambition; because we are freer to allot our time as we choose; because we were reared in a less hurried and more personal era; precisely, indeed, because our own lives are restricted and winding down—for all these reasons, we old could learn to offer the priceless gift of rapt attention.

People of all ages starve for this treasure that only another person can give. Finding oneself is a tedious task that seldom can be done without the patient, fascinated help of some caring other person. In today's hurried struggle to achieve, too few people are able to focus fixedly on another person's raw concerns. Among many acquaintances, often there is no one in whom we can confide.

If I would do for others what had been done for

me, I had much to learn. True listening is both a skill and an art. It demands the kind of vital attention that artists give their subjects as they paint. A shift in one's consciousness from self to the other self must take place.

I learned that guidelines for listening were being taught in the media and in schools and churches— because listening was thought to be a disappearing skill. I was warned not to give advice or point the way, but simply to enable others to find their own resources. I was taught not to listen for words so much as for feelings—needs, anger, and fear. These are revealed less in what is said than in tones and halftones, in hesitations and in a sudden speeding up of speech or movement.

I was shown how to share myself, so others could lose their fear of sharing. I was told what kinds of questions to ask when attempts at confiding are made, and how to respond when a confidence is given. I learned to listen with my eyes. Smarting wounds are often hidden under brave assurances. "I'm fine—never better," the jovial rejoinder rolls forth, while the person's eyes show only pain. I was told to watch for patterns. Bits of behavior, facial expressions, combinations of words, and inflections of voice slip into place—and in their configuration, a message is suddenly made clear.

Painful wisdom resulted when I learned to listen to myself. I saw habits unconsciously designed to keep others at arms length. A favorite was a hasty reassurance. When a person shared a problem, I would quickly point out the bright side, or proclaim no need to worry. This, I learned, is a way of washing our hands of the whole distressing mess. Empathy is needed to bridge the loneliness of pain. A perceptive sufferer feels abandoned, not comforted, by our cheeriness on his or her behalf.

I learned from observation that even prayer can be used as an escape from involvement. When a prayer group member tries to share some shattering loss, before the story is fully told and the relief of sharing gained, some other member often cuts in with, "Let's pray about it right now!" To protest the haste would be thought irreverent. But what of St. Paul's admonition, "Bear one another's burdens, and so fulfill the law of Christ" (Gal. 6:2)? I don't believe that prayer was meant to be a bolting exit.

I tried—and failed—to convince myself that at least I was never guilty of another popular ploy: trying to top a sufferer's sad story by telling about my own, worse problem.

"I know exactly how you feel," I would say (as if anyone ever knows exactly how another feels), "Once somebody backed into my car in a parking lot. Only mine was totaled. At least yours can be fixed. I was just sick over it. I loved that little car. . . ."!

As I studied, practiced and observed, a new world of listening began to round out. I became aware that I had been mishearing all my life. By taking words too much at face value, I had missed the message behind the words. Often the message is far different from the words—sometimes even opposite.

For example, if Jack says, "I'm not worried about it," each time a certain problem arises, when no one has asked if he is, the chances are he is worried about it. Also, he'll probably be defensive if you point this out. Hasn't his message all along been that he wants to think he isn't worried?

A way to help might be to say, "Why aren't you worried, Jack? I'd be." That lets him know you think worrying is natural. And in an effort to explain why he isn't worried, he may realize that he is. Admitting this may free him to seek solutions.

I used to go through life surrounded by a soundproof wall. Countless messages were wordlessly shouted to me by my husband, children, and friends. Through my unhearing ears, opportunities for sharing were lost that could have led to healing for us all.

But I knew now that I mustn't let the rivers of memory erode my present victories. It was more important that the soundproof wall was crumbling at last. The rewards of freedom could be mine. Through listening, I could enable others to move toward wholeness. And the reward for me would be a glowing heart.

A new dimension was being added to my life. A sense of belonging goes with putting one's ear to other people's hearts. I felt completed as a human being when I was asked to hear deep joys, pains, hopes, and fears.

Often I was inadequate, even helpless, in the face of great needs. I ached with the knowledge that someone who sought help was let down by my impotence. Yet even in my failure, the person knew I was there, reaching out, offering all I had, and would have given more if I had it to give. Since all caring is of God, the message of presence is always a message of his presence. Sometimes, mysteriously, I was given just the right words to say. Peace would creep into a troubled face, or a look of courage would begin to shine. In the person's eyes I would see our Lord look out. And I would know that I had served well. We two had sought each other in his name, and he was there in our midst.

"Partners in Giving"

For many years before I moved to Arlington, I had believed that there were special things for me to learn, do, and be to fulfill a plan for serving. This belief showered my daily activities with purpose and meaning. It gave me a solid, good feeling about myself and a steadfast sense of belonging. It was also among the treasures that were shattered in my collision with the new theology. Now, one by one, these treasures were being restored.

At times, through the mists, I almost glimpsed the niche I thought was designed for me. I almost heard the faint echo of a message for me that made my inner senses tingle. What was my special function within the body of humanity? Would I ever know? Or was my search itself that function?

I wanted to put my shoulder more effectively to other people's wheels. I had been taught that serving is our primary assignment. I knew from personal experience that helping others is the only way to truly belong to the human family. We are created as members of one body. When we fail to contribute to the welfare of another, we separate ourselves from the circulatory system, the nerve impulses, and the energy of the whole. When we opt for non-service, we condemn ourselves to internal isolation.

I began a dogged search for the special services I was created to render and for how I could fulfill my personhood by performing those services well. The search drew me toward the mentally ill and critically ill. And when I accepted that call, an important truth met me face to face: no natural gulf is fixed between ourselves and persons in these states. We alone, through our inadequacies and stupidities, create the seeming gulfs. For we are all—healthy and ill—just people, contending sometimes poorly, sometimes well, with whatever pain or problem is current in our lives. And always it is better to struggle not in isolation but together.

When Esther, who was a member of my church, had a breakdown, I visited her twice a week in the hospital's mental ward. She believed that years ago she had been transported, against her will, from another world to this one.

"I'm frantically lonely here," she would say with intensity. "You see, I'm so different from the people in this world that they don't want me around. They're quite, quite afraid of me—just because I came from out there!" She would wave her arm disjointedly to indicate how far away her place of origin was.

This sounded eerie. When Esther tried to talk about the problem of not belonging here, her friends and family understandably changed the subject with haste. She would then withdraw into herself and say nothing for the rest of their visit.

After seeing her several times, my dull wits began to make some obvious connections between my own experience and hers. I grasped the fact that solid truth lay behind her delusion. So I resolved to address that truth, bypassing the overlying muddle. I knew her diagnosis was schizophrenia. In a sense, she did come from another world. Others did fear and avoid her. Even her own family shrank back when she spoke of her deepest concerns. But her crazy babblings actually amounted to a kind of allegory, an allegory that set forth poignant experiences which she was striving to ease through sharing. And we normal ones so tragically lacked listening skills that we could not hear her straightforward message behind her senseless words!

When I began to take her seriously, our relationship became real. I could enter into her painful concerns and discuss her actual predicament of loneliness and exile. I treasure the day when she told me she was much less lonely now—because she had a friend.

My experience with Esther highlighted the truth that to be a friend, we must take the other person seriously. Failure to take one another seriously is what Dr. Alex Comfort calls "unpeopling" persons. Not to take others seriously for any reason whatever is to break the fragile cord of communication upon which all relationships depend. Discounting, condescending, and sidestepping issues have no place in friendship, whether the friend is despairing, angry, "crazy," ill, or dying.

Unpeopling may be the most besetting of all our sins against each other. As I noted earlier, we do it to minorities—the black, the foreign, the old, the handicapped, the mentally and emotionally sick, the physically sick, the dying. We unpeople children, teen-agers, our parents, even our husbands and wives. Unpeopling is a cruel way of severing others from us and pushing them into exile.

As I worked among the very ill and dying, I discovered that unpeopling them is an almost universal practice, a hallmark of our day. It used to be assumed that special insights and wisdom were imparted to persons who looked back over their lives, knowing their hours of giving and receiving were winding down. Friends and relatives gathered round, listening more earnestly than ever before to everything they said.

Today, the critically ill head the list of nonpersons. They are thrust into intensive care units, lonely rooms, or hospital beds with bleak white curtains round them. Friends, relatives, sometimes even nurses and doctors, see themselves as reassuring when they discount tortured outpourings from the hearts of the critically ill. "Don't you worry your head about your family. They'll manage all right," and "Stop putting yourself down. I don't believe you wasted your life." and "Now, now, you shouldn't think such things! You're going to be just fine!" are typical of replies heard in sickrooms.

Sometimes the despair of exile is clearly written in the ill person's eyes as a costly effort to confide deep fears falls impotently to the well-scrubbed floor. Yet it isn't hard to reach out a hand and pull the isolated person into a sense of caring, earnestly listening fellowship. It's as easy to say, "Why do you think so?" and "How do you feel about it?" and "How can we help?" as it is to say, "Don't talk like that!" Asking those questions provides a chance to share thoughts and burdens too heavy to bear alone. And it gives us who listen a chance to help.

Besides learning from others as I served them, I also learned by looking inside myself. At first, my chief objective was to be more conscious of when I was meeting the real needs of others and when I was only gratifying my own need to give. I thought of my satisfaction in serving as irrelevant. Wasn't the whole purpose to promote the other person's satisfaction?

But as I worked more and more with hard cases, I began to see that view as mindless legalism: thou shalt not enjoy! It served no practical purpose in anyone's welfare. On the contrary, it reduced satisfaction for the served as well as for the server. Moreover, without the sustaining help of satisfaction and pleasure, one soon becomes drained and exhausted in difficult and painful kinds of work. I saw new meaning in the admonition, "Do not be grieved, for the joy of the Lord is your strength" (Neh. 8:10) and in Jesus' assurance that it is joyful to give.

Looking back, my early attitude toward self-gratification in serving reminds me of the attitude toward sex of the women in my mother's generation. In those days, the woman was assumed to be the only giver and the man the only receiver of all physical pleasure in sex. If she got any pleasure, it was supposed to be the purified joy of giving the man she loved what he wanted. As a result, she felt guilty and unladylike if she had normal reactions and often developed blocks and a sense of martyrdom about sex. So, naturally, the man's pleasure was short-circuited, too. Marital sex was often a grim duty for both partners, executed for the sole purpose of producing children.

Some Christians get themselves in this kind of bind about good works. If they admit to themselves that they are meeting their own deep needs when they offer sacrificial service, they feel ashamed. But if they don't admit it, and instead play a dutiful self-sacrificial role, they spoil their services for the served as well as for themselves.

I felt wonderfully liberated when I ceased seeing a strong personal need to give as a dubious motive for giving. There is nothing at all wrong with wanting to give—provided one does not let that need stand in the way of giving *only needed and desired* service to others. There is the rub. We often let our own need to serve overrule another's need for independence. And that is a kind of rape. It has the qualities of physical rape. It is painful, humiliating, and destructive. I had never thought of myself as a rapist. But now I had to face the fact that I often had attempted rape. If I didn't succeed, it was only because my intended victims were too strong for me. My behavior with Sadie and Estelle mentioned earlier is an example.

My choice of metaphors is no accident. I believe that our built-in need to give is one of the beautiful, ingenious gifts included in creation, like having two sexes with equal need for one another. Some psychologists might say that all giving and receiving only symbolizes the sex act. I doubt it. Something in me says that the sex act is the symbol. I suspect that physical sex stands like a monument to the enormous universal truth that if you have something another person needs, desires, and will accept, and you give it, both you and the one you serve will have joy and be fulfilled.

My deepening awareness of my own intense need to give helped me to see that serving others is one part of an inescapable partnership. We give by receiving as surely as by giving we receive. The relationship of serving and being served falls far short of what it was created to be, unless both partners have shared pleasure and satisfaction in its accomplishment.

When I grasped the full implications of this truth, I felt as if a door had swung silently open and I were standing breathlessly in the doorway of the kingdom of God. It is a kingdom that is intended to be ours. It can be ours, if only we set aside our countless pretenses, small and large. Then, we can live honestly and simply in the joy of the Lord that is our strength.

In the light of that insight, I saw that what had most often dismayed and defeated me, dissipated my energy, wasted my time, and dampened my heart was my unconscious, meaningless, merry-go-round effort to maintain status in my own and other people's eyes. Without that self-defeating practice, known as pride, I could face my own needs directly without subterfuge. I could give, knowing that I was thereby receiving, and I could easily and freely love, because I knew I was loved.

"Who Only Stand and Cheer"

As I probed for human needs and how to fill them, I suddenly saw that we also serve who only stand and cheer! The possibilities for such a service seemed almost boundless. It soon multiplied itself in mini-ministries, each with a small gift of new wholeness for me and others.

These ministries are good news especially for the old, whose almost daily bad news is that there are fewer and fewer contributions they can make. Regardless of one's growing dependence on many kinds of help—often even because of it—one can exercise the ministry of applause. Professionals and volunteers in the field of helping need as much as anyone else to be encouraged, confirmed in who they are, and given constructive feedback on what they do and how they do it. There is no one who doesn't need these heartening services. And always there are too few who deliver them.

Of all the helping vocations, the ministry of the applause may be most neglected. Fearful perhaps of fostering conceit, we tend to say to others, "Isn't Cindy wonderful?" rather than tell her directly, "Cindy, you're wonderful!" We pay for that pattern in times of grief. "I never told Dad how proud of him I was. Now it's too late." "I always meant to tell her how much she helped us all. Oh, if I only had!"

One reason for our failure is the fear of sounding gushy, mushy, or insincere. Another is misplaced concern for how praise might make the person feel. The best answer to that last excuse was given by an effective young clergyman.

"I've a good compliment for you, Jerry," I said, "but I'm afraid it'll embarrass you."

"Come on, tell me," he replied with startling honesty. "Even if it does, I'll remember it afterwards."

I have locked those words among my treasures of wisdom.

It isn't true that very competent people need no reassurance. Common companions of outstanding performance are over-sensitivity and self-doubt. Superior persons tend to set impossible standards for themselves, inevitably fall short, then suffer the same pangs of failure endured by a chronic lout.

Although the truly famous get praise enough, non-famous gifted people are among the most deprived minorities. An unbroken line of reassurance is often needed to help them fulfill their huge potential, while we—assuming they need no reassurance—offer them less than we do ordinary people. Yet unless sideline cheers force them to recognize that they score high with observers, even though they disappoint themselves, they become disheartened. All of us are then the losers.

This is not to imply that ordinary people don't need applause as much as the gifted, but only that the gifted need it no less. We all excel in some way sometimes. Cheers when we do well build the needed confidence to excel again. I suspect that many aptitudes implanted in us never bear fruit because when we first try them out, we think no one considers them worthwhile.

Biofeedback has demonstrated that we acquire skill and function more easily if we are informed at once when we do well. Psychiatrist Eric Berne called feedback from others "strokes" and said that if we lack our share of stroking, our "spinal columns shrivel." I think he's right. With good feedback, my successes double. With none, the simplest task becomes a burden.

Failure to applaud excellence is a kind of theft. It robs others of the energy, confidence, and incentive that approval brings. Without that nourishment, God-given endowments will not reach their maximum effectiveness. Our failure to applaud also robs others of their joy in what they offer. And it robs the rest of us of the fruits that would have resulted had applause been given.

Granted, there is some hazard in applause. But that is true of all good things. Even prayer can become a bolting exit. Shall we therefore cease to pray? Sincere confirming can drift into flattery. Must we therefore cease to reinforce the best? Instead, we can keep in mind that flattery is an insult and can be quite destructive, while honest, confirming feedback is power and lubrication.

If we dislike giving direct applause, there is a twin ministry that can be carried on behind closed doors. It lacks the stimulation of personal interaction but offers the satisfaction of seeing that just rewards are given. It consists of watching in all directions for good performance on the job. When we see it, we then send a note describing it to the person's employer, personnel manager or whoever controls hiring, promotions and pay raises.

Sample: "Dear Mr. (Ms.). . . : Today I witnessed the kind of service from one of your employees that has become a rarity in our world. Under very trying conditions [state them: heat, cold, confusion, pressure, another's anger etc.] John Jones continued to perform his duties with efficiency and consideration [care and courtesy . . . speed, skill, and concern . . . kindness and authority . . . patience and firmness . . . or whatever]. This is the kind of service that is deeply appreciated. I congratulate you on your good judgment in selecting and instructing your personnel.

Sincerely,"

Footnote on human nature: If we give our addressee his or her cut of the credit, the chances of the employee being rewarded are improved.

The effect of such a letter can be substantial. Sometimes we get no reply and may never know the result—an example of no feedback! But often we receive an appreciative note saying that a copy of our letter was given to the person and was also placed as a permanent record in his or her personnel file. Twice I was told that in addition to that, copies of the letters had been sent to the chain store's national headquarters. Once I learned that as a result of my letter, the shoe clerk I had praised was being honored for her good service at a party given by the store. And once a police chief wrote me that the young officer I had seen performing well was new to the force and that therefore my observations were particularly significant and helpful.

Once, on a bus, a woman blasted the driver for a narrowly missed accident that was not his fault. He remained calm and courteous throughout her tirade, even though she would not let him explain what had really happened. She ended by saying she would report him for careless driving, a threat she repeated when she disembarked.

I told him I didn't agree with her and asked if he was worried.

"Yes, ma'am, I am," he said sadly. "The company really comes down on any kind of carelessness. My job's not worth nothing right now. And we got a baby on the way!"

I wrote the bus company, giving my version of the incident. I said our driver, far from almost causing an accident, had shown both caution and skill in averting one, and that afterward he had shown unusual ability in controlling himself under the additional stress of the woman's accusation.

I rarely ride buses, and I thought no more about the incident until a couple of years later. Then, as I mounted a bus, a voice warm with feeling greeted me by name.

"You don't remember me, but I remember you! You saved my job. I'm grateful—hear!"

Replies to letters of commendation often reiterate one sad point. Amid a downpour of criticism and complaint, they say, a drop of praise is rare. This fact gives our words the power of rarity and multiplies their force. No wonder heartening reactions often occur! The results of well-placed applause remind me of the old Red Cross Bloodbank slogan: "Give a pint and save a life!" A few minutes spent in speaking or writing a constructive evaluation of a person's behavior may one day bear more fruit than anything else we have done.

Besides, it's fun.

21

"The Living Rock"

My need for the church outweighed the bewildering pain she caused me.
But I couldn't live with the pain.

Long ago I learned that it helps with a dilemma to find out more about what caused it. Perhaps my yearning for a church home was just another outmoded hope. I decided to leave St. Luke's with her unbearable conflicts and devote myself to seeing how other parishes dealt with the new theology.

Within easy driving distance there happened to be many churches of my own denomination and others. Most big churches have several Sunday services besides adult discussion and study groups during the week. I could dip into the lives of several parishes concurrently. Comparing them yielded fascinating discoveries.

I learned that most denominations are far from the monolithic institutions I had imagined. More and greater differences in beliefs exist between individual churches and individual members within a denomination than exist between most denominations. The great religious unrest that peaked in the humanistic and now defunct God-Is-Dead explosion may have intensified differences that ordinarily are mild. But whatever the cause, in parish after parish I saw people aligning themselves with one or another of three major persuasions that cut across denominational lines.

Persuasion A stresses that the living church must be flexible, keep abreast of scientific discoveries and cultural changes, focus on human needs, and ensure that these needs are met by social action. Only then can she spread the gospel of God's astounding love.

Persuasion B stresses the opposite. Amid the feverish vacillations of our day, the enduring church must remain centered in her time-honored doctrines and traditions and must maintain her identity as an institution apart from the world. Only then can her message carry weight.

Persuasion C stresses that the church must teach all people to focus on Jesus Christ as their personal friend, counselor, Lord, and Savior who speaks directly to each heart. A personal relationship with him is all that matters. The less time spent on anything else the better. Only in fellowship with him can one do anything of value.

Later, I learned that these persuasions and various combinations of them have invaded theologians' minds, captured the headlines about religion, and thrown lay people into turmoil throughout Christian history. Their co-existence has mothered major conflicts and schisms and stimulated great personalities and saints. The church zigzags her way through history, grasping and teaching first one interpretation of the Christian enterprise, then another.

That may be well. Such changes force us to plumb the depths of our faith instead of taking it for granted. They keep the message sharp, vigorous, shocking—as it was when it first burst on complacent minds.

As I observed these persuasions in action, however, they appeared to be merely conflicting powers on my doorstep. I felt only dismay that the core leadership of A, B, and C each regarded people of their persuasion as the only true Christians, with the others more a threat than a witness to the gospel. I thought that horrifying. In the secular world, members of one persuasion cheerfully concede that members of other professions also are useful citizens. It was embarrassing that Christians could not do as well. (Actually, the analogy breaks down because secular professionals, while tolerant of other professions, are no more magnanimous about different persuasions within their own profession than Christians are!)

At this point, a familiar bell began to toll sadly along my vertebra. Just before I left St. Luke's, how had I felt about the Rev. Joseph Lox, his wife Sue, and the famous seminar leader, Dr. Trigg? As staunch supporters of Persuasion A, they had considered people like me a threat to the church's survival. And I had returned the compliment!

There was even less excuse for me than for them, because at various times I had identified with all three persuasions. When the fire of the gospel first burned in me, I acted out my commitment in terms of Persuasion A. I felt strangled by too many sterile affirmations and had little choice but to meet the Lord in social action. There alone I could see how passionately real and singing with life he is.

Later, I learned that the martyrdom which overt action inevitably incurs is unbearable without more inner life than Persuasion A can offer. Through struggles, ordeals and prayers, I found my way into Persuasion C. In my confusion and despair, I could see Christ best among the intense new evangelicals, where faith runs deep and swift, its banks rocklike and narrow, and certainty is a rushing torrent sweeping all questions aside.

Then, I thought I held both halves of the precious sphere of Christian truth. I still believed Persuasion B was mere dry bones—brick, mortar, ritual, and the letter of the law. But when I suffered "future shock" from swift changes in my life and the culture I knew, I could discern him best in the traditional body of the church. As my old life disintegrated, leaving me without the shelter of familiar structures, I knew that Persuasion B also is necessary for Christian wholeness. There, God symbolized in stability, permanence, and a quiet forward march toward goals that, like himself, are the same yesterday, today, and tomorrow.

Where did that leave me today? Who was I in the Christian faith? Something peaceful, yet exciting, now began to happen to my vision of the church. She became less a thing to be grasped than to be loved. I saw her with the kind of eyes used in seeing works of art. I perceived that strands from all persuasions belong in the Christian tapestry. The paradoxical interweaving of sharply contrasting threads makes the fabric of faith brilliant and enduring in the heart.

I saw how the Lord of history pervades his earth and how only a tiny area of him is seen by each of us because he is so high and wide and deep. I reread 1 Corinthians 12:14-26 and saw how truly it speaks to the many persuasions of the Christian faith. "If the whole body were an eye, where would be the hearing? If the whole body were an ear, where would be the sense of smell? . . . The eye cannot say to the hand, 'I have no need of you,' nor again the head to the feet, 'I have no need of you.' . . . God has so composed the body, . . . that there may be no discord . . . If one member suffers, all suffer together. . . ."

I felt my sense of belonging in the church gently seep back into me. As the comfort of it gave me new wholeness, I saw the contrasting experiences of my past as a chain of mini-resurrections. I knew that life itself repeats with a rhythmic beat the symbols of God's plan. Not only is the Resurrection message written eternally in history with Christ's death and his leap to new being, but it is written also in everything God made. I could see it in how the brightness of aging stars is slowly sucked into their depths until the stars become great black holes of death—then the brightness is exploded outward in a glorious blaze of new light. I could see it in the rhythmic warmth of spring that brings blossoms and fruit from frozen, barren ground. I could see it in other persons. I could even see it in myself in the bright, warm rise of hope, new seeking, and new struggle that had come to me after the desolation of each experience of despair.

As the vision of God's omnipresence pulled my life together, I felt strengthened, quickened, quieted, and warmed. I knew who I was and where I stood in the church. Despite her many contradictions, she had continued to be leaven in the heavy dough of all my striving. Though no better than the rest of us, she is like a distinguished professor of mathematics who cannot keep his checkbook balanced. He still teaches others the truths on which all science rests. It is the church that falls short, not what she stands for. And it is in her stand, not in herself, that her value lies.

I looked for and found a church of my denomination that comfortably maintained a healthy, lively balance of all three persuasions. And soon I was to require the strength, courage, and support that came from a renewed sense of belonging in a church that was my home.

"Despise Not the Chastening"

It was now thirteen years after I moved to Arlington intent on starting a new life, twelve after the church's new theology exploded in the God-Is-Dead outcry and eight after I cried out from the depths of despair for help—and received it.

Those last eight years had been the richest of my life. My sense of belonging, contributing, loving, and being loved were restored. My sense of progress had zoomed to an all-time high. My sense of autonomy, security, and power were at normal levels. My sense of accomplishment was a bubbling spring. My coping skills were steadier, my goals clearer, and the meaning of life better understood than ever before. Never had I been so well-equipped to live with total zest.

Then my world began to fall apart.

I don't believe we are created to lead tranquil lives. Biologists tell us that species cease to evolve when their environments lack stress. Recent experiments show that individual animals, too, fail to develop well when stress is absent. And throughout my own life, growth and understanding increased whenever trouble came. Beginning in the spring, a series of

[*183*]

malignant events overtook me that were unlike any I had experienced. I had no grooves to help me through them. Assailed by poorly comprehended kinds of pain, my vaunted network of guidelines and solutions dimmed and grew hard to follow.

I thought I couldn't bear it when I learned the fate of Frank, my favorite cousin. He had been a man of marvelous gifts of laughter, of appreciation, of teaching, of sharing, of stimulating the imagination, of affection, and of relating to small children. Nine years my senior, he had laced my childhood with his exuberance and love. He taught me zest in learning. He taught me to appreciate animals with tenderness and humor. Even when I was very small, he made me feel fully human and entitled to all the deference personhood deserves.

Christened Frank Stringfellow Barr, my cousin dropped the Frank in his twenties and was generally known either as Stringfellow or Winkie Barr.

He had a disciplined and sparkling mind that had brought him many honors in school and throughout a long career. An internationally known educator, editor, lecturer, and promoter, he was also the author of eleven books, some of them monumental in size and scholarship.

Now, at eighty-two, his shining mind had so dimmed that he could not even care for himself. He was brought to his native Virginia and placed in the physical assistance unit of a church-sponsored retirement community near me.

I resisted the diagnosis of senile dementia, knowing that quite curable conditions are often misdiagnosed as senility. I had read of cases where good medical attention, plus mental stimulation and interaction with people who cared, had restored diminished mental faculties. Resolving to make this happen with Frank, I focused my energy and thought on retrieving his mind.

He had always enjoyed clothes. I took him shopping to replenish his neglected wardrobe. He loved music and art. I took him to concerts and galleries. He loved nature and exercise. I took him on long walks through parks and along streams. In bad weather, I took him driving through lovely country scenes and fascinating, quaint streets. I took him to the best specialists for physical and mental evaluations. I worked with him in the small garden plot the home assigned to him. I toiled and worried, hoped, prayed, and struggled. But a growing sense of futility about my huge investment menaced me. In a few hours at most, everything that happened to Frank vanished in the mists of his mind.

One evening I telephoned to remind him that in twenty minutes I would pick him up to take him to a concert. When I arrived at his room door, I found that he had undressed and gone to bed.

"Why didn't you tell me we were going, so I could be ready?" he asked.

"Well, you know how easily things slip our minds," I replied tactfully.

He smiled in forgiveness. "Yes, we all forget sometimes," he said kindly.

Since all happenings and conversations were written in water for Frank, a connected conversation was impossible. But on a moment-to-moment basis, he was often painfully perceptive. One of his confusions was that he easily lost track of whom he was talking to, and the habit sometimes forced me to eavesdrop.

"My little cousin was here a few minutes ago," he

told me one day. "She's helpful and very dependable, but not very intelligent."

By his standard of a trained and disciplined mind, he was totally right. So I praised his accuracy without calling attention to his oversight. Thus, he felt good about his discernment, while I felt healthily humble.

He kept me self-aware in other ways, as well. When I did anything for him that he particularly enjoyed, if he recalled the occasion at all, he often credited it to someone else.

"Alex took me to the most delightful concert this afternoon," he announced as I drove him home following that concert. "I wish you had been there. It was magnificent."

To my consternation, I felt discounted and cheated of my rightful appreciation.

Belief that Frank could be cured sustained me through all my struggles to help him. I had read that severe loss of mental function can result not only from curable disease but also from depression and grief. Frank was a man of close, deep, lasting relationships. He had always been fiercely loyal to and strongly dependent on his family and friends. These characteristics had given him a life rich in people. They had also made him highly vulnerable to the many shattering griefs he had suffered in his old age. Perhaps the griefs had driven him to draw the curtain on unbearable memories and to inadvertently shut out memory itself. Behind the drawn curtain, perhaps his mind was resting quietly, brilliant and healthy as ever—awaiting only a knowing hand to pull the curtain back.

I took him to a renowned geriatric specialist and asked for a complete evaluation of his condition. After several visits and extensive physical and psychological examinations, I was informed that Frank had Alzheimer's disease—"a progressive, irreversible, organic brain syndrome." In everyday language, Frank was incurable. Only further deterioration was in store.

I was stunned, then agonized, then totally spent. All I could think of was that now I must watch Frank's once extraordinary mind continue to decompose. I doubted that I was equal to it. The message it sent threatened to undermine all the ground I had gained in my slow climb back to well being. Anxieties I had hoped were long ago rooted out rushed back. Every normal bit of forgetfulness or oversight in myself became a symptom. Old age stereotypes I had thought vanquished hung about my shoulders like a wet cloak.

It was useless to recall the extensive recent research revealing that genuine senile dementia is rare and that healthy, active old people have little cause for apprehension concerning it. One personal experience outweighs a carload of documented facts. For me, Frank's case was not rare; it was my whole horizon. If senile dementia plundered his disciplined, brilliant mind, how could I hope my lesser faculties would not soon be its victim?

A profound sense of personal failure sharpened the teeth of the pain and fear that tore me. When we go all out to do something and fail, even if we know the task to be impossible, we feel worthless. This was a large factor in the epidemic of suicides that followed the stock market crash in the Great Depression of 1929. No individual could have prevented the crash, and no one could help suffering losses when it came. Yet each breadwinner who had invested heavily in the market felt that somehow he personally was responsible for his family's sudden privation. *He* was a failure. *He* had let his trusting family down. Because I had committed myself to saving Frank's mind, even though the medical report stated that his disease was irreversible and progressive, I felt I had failed. Worse! I had failed him, when he had helped me so much as a child.

In the weeks that followed, I struggled to use my trusted guidelines as a means of escape from my returning old despair and from a sick new fear of mental decay. But I saw myself as only endlessly shaking the bars of the ever-shrinking cell of old age. I must accept Frank's condition—but how could I accept a thing like that? I must change what I could—but I seemed powerless to change anything that really mattered! I must focus on the present— but it was the present that strangled my hope!

The first faint paling of my darkness came with the slowly rising hope that seemingly fruitless struggles are not, in fact, fruitless at all. Inner problems are often sorted out as we thrash about. Strengthening and stretching of mental muscles go on as we resist despair. Our hearts and minds are readied to grasp new insights and opportunities. *New!* That was what I needed—the unpredictable inbreaking of healing and new life, such as I had experienced eight years ago when I was pulled from the depths!

This time the healing did not come at the moment of insight. But a few weeks later, in the most unexpected and unlikely form, an inbreaking did occur. And when it came, it brought a new way of seeing my situation that enabled me to contend once more.

I was not successful in holding back the slow tide of oblivion that engulfed Frank's mind. But my attitude toward my role in his life was new. Now I saw him as the giver, myself as his apprentice. Instead of fighting to find strength and time to provide the emotional support, entertainment, and exercise he needed, I found myself wondering what I would learn from him that day. Instead of seeing his limitations as pathetic, I saw them as my chance to learn how to hear the messages and feelings behind the often tangled thicket of his thoughts and words. The tragedy of his memory loss faded. Instead, I felt gratitude that his aching griefs were thus mercifully dissolved.

I could see also that the wiping away of memory allowed him to experience long-familiar beauties as though they were fresh from the hand of God. When we came on our walks to blooming honeysuckle, a bed of wild violets or a little waterfall, he would cry out like a child, "Oh, look at that!" as though nothing like it had ever been seen. Although the past faded with accelerating speed, his responses to the present moment were perceptive and poetic. In some ways, they were even more piercing as his vocabulary disappeared and he expressed sensitive observations in simple, childish words.

One day, with his eyes moving along the grass at the path's edge, he said, "Those tiny little yellow flowers are like sparks in the very green. They look up at us without ever looking down. I think they expect us to be so glad to see them that we show it on our faces. And maybe they're right."

Of trees blowing in the wind, he said: "They're friendly and so beautiful. They wave to us and bow, yet they don't flatter. They're always themselves, not phony. They like to reach up and up and say, 'Here we are, and here you are. We like you and hope you like us.' I can tell them, 'Yes, I do.' Can you?"

I said I could.

Of squirrels he said, "They have an air of knowing what they want."

I had not noticed that truth about squirrels, but I could see at once that they are not at all like rabbits, who appear uncertain, or like birds, who seem engaged in some kind of internal debate.

"Those little roads"—he meant paths—"that are running through the tall trees are happy because they're free to go where they like." How perfectly that definition caught the winding charm of the un-planned small trails that took their own ways among the towering poplar and crouching laurel on the steep hillside.

Of a patch of dandelions he said, "Aren't they lovely? They're just there—and sort of solid. I think they're saying, 'Don't get in our way; we just want to be!'"

Whenever I see dandelions now, I know he was right.

He fell instantly in love with all small children. At the very sight of a child in the distance, his voice and face grew soft. Once he exclaimed, "It's the littleness that makes it wonderful." Later while we walked beside my oasis brook (which he called "our river") as it turned and rippled round bends and over rocks, he said, "It's just like little kids. It knows what it wants to do and goes ahead and does it."

As his area of thinking became smaller, he somehow maintained the contours and grace of a keen and cultured mind. I noted, fascinated, that his character and personality were unaltered by his dissolving ability to think. Although he no longer knew who anyone was, he related to all persons with courteous charm. He often had exuberant exchanges with nurses and other staff members at the home. They understood him and loved him for his politeness and warmth. That filled him with joy. For he knew instantly when he was loved.

His sense of values and ethics, as well as esthetics, was unmarred. He even retained his sense of obligation as a citizen and never missed an opportunity to make the world a better place. On our walks, he liked to pick up trash along the way, and he applauded my practice of taking along a big paper bag to put it in. We would dump it in the park trash cans. With courtly deference, he would approach any person within twenty-five feet of one of these cans and say, "I beg your pardon for troubling you, but do you object to my putting this trash in your can?" He also asked permission to pick up "your trash" when anyone was nearby.

I found it heartening that such warm gifts of the spirit as deference and a wish to make the world a better place had more endurance than the chillier endowment of a rational mind.

Indeed, of all the learnings I gained from Frank, the one I treasure most is the discovery that our vaunted powers of reason are not the mark of humanness. Frank was as fully human now as he was when he was celebrated for his ability to stimulate thousands of other minds through his sparkling lectures and written words.

Can it be said that humanity is what remains when we are stripped of all our tools? Logic and memory are necessary for building civilization, science, systems of thought, of values, and even of faith. How could we possibly understand our world without memory or logic? And yet with scarcely a shred of either, Frank still met his world with understanding. He proved in his person that one can be truly human without the most honored powers of the mind.

It is not so much our ability to reason as how we respond to our world that makes us human. Frank was moved by music, art, humor, natural beauty, and all the higher qualities of humankind. He reacted fully to them with his whole person, his face, his voice tones, his movements, his childlike verbal images. When I consider the vast riches his personality still offered as his mind dimmed out, I know that the most important of the many things he taught me is a new grasp of what being fully human means.

"The Scent of Water"

A quotation from Job 14:7-9 was often in my mind in the early months of my ministry to Frank. I hoped and believed that the once towering tree of his mind would sprout again. When I learned this was not to be, I strove to apply the words of comfort to myself: "For there is hope for a tree, if it be cut down, that it will sprout again, and that its shoots will not cease. Though its root grow old in the earth, and its stump die in the ground, yet at the scent of water it will bud and put forth branches like a young plant."

But the series of malignant events referred to earlier hit me with such force that I felt myself crumple.

At the peak of my anxiety over Frank, I lost another beloved member of my family. And while that grief still gripped me, my hearing suddenly dulled to the point where conversation was a strain. It seemed that one by one the doors to life's treasures were being shut in my face. With the steady ache of too many losses haunting my nights and days, I called my doctor, poured my story into his ear and—for the first time in my life—asked for a tranquilizer. That night and the next, I slept in peace.

But on the third day, I rebelled at chemical solutions. Surely I was created with equipment to deal with stresses by natural means! One of my sons had often urged me to start jogging. It was widely reputed as a relaxer, calmer and general health builder, he said. Untempted, I had always replied that I needed none of those things. Now I needed them all. I donned comfortable shoes and headed for my oasis.

The area had finally been developed by the county. The natural waterfall and privacy were gone, but the rapids, moss covered boulders, and tall trees with their own songs and the songs of birds were still umarred. Graded and equipped with an asphalt path connecting it with other parks, the place was ideal for jogging.

I was seventy-two and not expecting to break marathon records. But embedded in my consciousness were pleasant memories of childhood sprints. With naïve confidence, I set off. I was not prepared for the reality of trying to run at three score years and twelve. It was as if a frequent childhood escape nightmare had returned. In the dream, I had fled pursuers through deep mire, my weary muscles barely able to lift my legs, heavy mud clutching at my feet. Now again, each foot felt encased in a twenty-pound shoe. After only a few steps, I panted like a dog in August.

The message was sinister: my eager spirit was trapped in a body too old for normal exercise! Such a possibility had never crossed my mind. I sank on a fallen log by the stream and forced my thoughts to surround the soft, free sound of tumbling water. I could not face the discovery that had rammed into me like a champion's fist. I would not believe I was corroded so by time that my useless muscles could no longer respond to my commands. My heart shouted, "No!"

My memory of easy running was so bright that present reality seemed a fraud. Every few days, I found myself retesting—jogging again the few steps I could. Did I only imagine it, or could I really take more steps than before? For the first time, I counted them. Only eighteen. But I was driven from within. A week later, I counted them again. Twenty-five! That was progress! What if I jogged twenty-five steps, then walked twenty-five, then jogged twenty-five again?

I tried it and found I could rest enough while walking to keep a chain of twenty-five-step links going for ten minutes or more. In a couple of weeks I had increased each link to fifty steps. I moved on to seventy-five, then one hundred. After that, I used the distance between telephone poles for links. Jogging became a wonderful addiction. I could not wait each day to get my foot in the path.

One glorious morning, I found that overnight— miraculously, mysteriously—the heaviness had disappeared. My feet felt almost airy, as if I were being wafted along. I was able to jog continuously! When tired, I could rest simply by jogging slower. Rapture swept me. The walls that had closed in fell away. I was free!

For most people their first runner's high may be a quiet joy. For me, it was a blaze of glory. Multiplied by my years, brightened by my never having heard of a runner's high, compounded by many messages that the old can hope only to slow down their deterioration, the experience shot across my dark horizon like the aurora borealis.

I saw that most of our old age shackles are simply the price we pay for the gloomy messages we buy. Now I could buy joyous messages instead: I wasn't winding down. I was in graduate school, learning to triumph over the myriad ills of old age. Even my muscles could grow stronger, more agile, and learn to do new things. Old age hadn't trapped my body; what had trapped it was my not using it as I should. I could undertake anything, knowing that if I practiced, I could improve. If even my ancient body was free to respond to my will, how much more were my mind and heart! My future was not gone; it was out there waiting to see what I would do.

On the wings of this experience, I was enabled to relax concerning Frank, contend with my growing deafness, adjust to my new grief and accept the uncertainty of life ahead. To neutralize brainwashing and produce an upsurge of hope and confidence, I had needed a triumphant experience. Facts gained secondhand through research are helpful in clarifying and reenforcing what we learn through pain, failure, struggle, and ultimate success. But it is only through our own experiences that truths are made a part of our viscera and bones.

In the months that followed my breakthrough to freedom, for the first time in my life, I felt the soft, tingling exhilaration of being physically fit. Although I had always worked hard and inadvertently had gotten some exercise that way, never before had I invested time in a program with the goal of body building. Now that I was training my body to fulfill what bodies are designed to do, I saw my world enlarge instead of shrink. I didn't even feel dependent on artificial transportation anymore. I knew that under my own steam, I could get where I needed to go.

I felt more alive as my seventy-fourth birthday rolled by than I had when I was young. Increasingly, I saw new possibilities that I myself and life contained. Long forgotten, uninhibited confidence surged in me again. I was my own woman!—in some ways more than ever before.

Better than that, I had been given another mini-resurrection. I had been raised, better than before, from the dead. Not only was this the reflection of a larger truth. It was also an affirmation of present existence. Vital things remained for me to learn, be, and do. Surely there must be purpose in my being given new life. I knew I must not let the Giver down.

"By Faith
We Have Peace"

When William McGaffin, a respected journalist and author in his mid-sixties, and Jean, his beautiful and strong-minded young wife, learned that his bone cancer was terminal, they resolved that he would not go to the hospital. He would remain home, surrounded by familiar possessions and cared for only by people who loved him. They were not trying to dodge the truth, they said—only to deal with it in ways that seemed right.

Bill, who had been named to the Columbia University journalism Hall of Fame, had served at various times as war correspondent, London bureau chief, European correspondent, United Nations correspondent, and Washington correspondent. Now, he was assistant chief of the *Chicago Daily News'* Washington bureau and was looking forward to retirement on his next birthday.

He had experienced a spiritual conversion two years ago, and he wanted me to tell him all I knew—and believed—about death and how to meet it. First, he asked for my thoughts on spiritual healing.

"I believe," I said, "that God is able and is good, and that his nature is to love us with every part of his infinite vastness, not with just a man-size piece of it. I think he can, and sometimes does, heal incurable illness. But I also think he can choose—*lovingly*—not to heal but to take the person where love got its start. And I think it's our task to accept, on faith, that his choice—whatever it may be—is a fuller expression of his nature, which is love, than the choice we prefer."

Bill said he found that view helpful. "I've prayed very hard for healing, but it hasn't come. People who insist that physical healing is invariably the will of God make me feel guilty for not being healed. I don't need that!"

We talked about the fact that death does not always come in peace and quietness but often in ugliness and pain. Bill said, "It seems a contradiction. Of love, I mean. How could love make death so hard?"

I said I saw the ugliness and pain as less a part of death itself than of the body holding too tightly to what it has—the pain of desire, of struggle, of fighting what seems evil to the body and clutching what seems good.

"I believe death reaches out with warm, not cold, hands to lift us where energy pulses on without the pain of resistance. I see love as pure energy, the source of all other energy. Unless the message of the New Testament is a fraud—and if it is, life is too meaningless to be worth living—it's only beyond this life that we sink fully into the love of God. And it's the warm hands of death that take us there."

We talked of how one can learn to relax about death and stop struggling. And that when this is done, the person has much less physical and emotional pain.

"It sounds great," Bill said, "but not very easy. And I'm too tired to do hard things. Dying makes me more tired than anything else I've ever tried. And I'm scared. And that makes me wonder how real my faith is."

So we talked of how the biological fear of death is no index of one's faith. I said I thought biological fear is an implanted part of every living creature, just as pain is.

"Both are God's insurance against our passively letting harm come to us. But in typically human fashion, we misuse safeguards. We run from pain, even when it's teaching us something important. And we fight death even when its designated time has come. It's normal, not faithless, to be scared; and it's downright upright to admit it, as you do. I don't think the Lord's a bit worried about our fears. He knows what to do with them."

"Thanks," Bill said. "That helps with the double-bind part. I was scared partly because I was scared."

One day when I arrived, Bill greeted me with a look of triumph. "I've got good news. I haven't been scared for three or four days!"

"That's great! I'm proud of you!" I cried in real excitement.

The way Bill beamed at my response would have convinced me, if I hadn't already known it, that dying people need praise as much as anyone.

Now Bill had another problem. "When I stopped being scared, grief hit me," he said. "I feel lonely. It's like everybody I know is dying. I don't want to leave them." His eyes filled.

I said I liked his tears, because they meant he wasn't bottling up.

As we talked about grief, I was impressed by the way he came to grips with it, and I told him so. "I particularly like the insight that you won't really lose the people you love—may even be closer to them. That rings bells. I'll pass it on to other people facing death."

"I'm glad," Bill said softly.

I told him that yesterday a woman had said she was helped by focusing on her friends and family she would soon see.

"That's a good one," Bill responded. "There're some people I've really missed. I'll work on it and let you know next time how I do."

"Don't forget the people you've yet to meet," I suggested. "How would you like to get in a huddle with King David. There was a man with an interesting life!"

One of the reasons Bill had been such a successful journalist was that he had always prepared for his assignments with hard homework. I wasn't surprised on my next visit to find he had reread all his favorite Bible stories in preparation for the interviews he intended to have shortly. I told him I could hardly wait to get my first copy of the *Eternal Daily Messenger* with one of his features in it.

"I'll save the best ones for you," he said. "Maybe they'll help you get acquainted with the right people."

One day when Bill's pain was great, I told him it helped me to think of death as an assignment. "You've got a tougher one than most. It's exciting to see the first-class job you're doing in carrying it out."

"Am I really doing a good job?" he whispered, looking pleased through his pain.

Later, when he felt better, he told me, "The assignment idea helps. It makes me feel I still have useful work to do, and that others care how I do it."

The dying have the same needs the healthy have. They are not a separate species. They want approval, a sense of contributing, and success in what they attempt just as the healthy do. Their essential humanity is unaltered. They differ from the rest of us only in that they won't be with us long.

Soon after Bill and I began to talk about death, he and Jean asked me to see if, in addition to our private meetings, three of their friends would agree to gather with us at his bedside each week as a support group. Bill wanted the gatherings to be times of prayer, Bible study, spiritual discussion, music, fellowship and Jean's good food; times of deep sharing, peace, joy and love that he and Jean could plan for and look forward to all week. We accepted the invitation with a sense of adventure, expecting sorrow from the experience but also bountiful gifts of broader understanding and deeper faith. We were not disappointed.

Though different in background and personality, we had common ground in our faith. This made a creative combination, and we worked well together.

Bill, with his journalistic training, offered thoughtful questions, well-focused insights and intellectual integrity as he sought to reconcile himself to death through faith. He made us wrestle with issues we might not otherwise have faced until the time when we, too, saw death striding toward us. He also offered the strength and inspiration that watching courage in action brings. Finally, he was a great partner in giving. He made us feel we contributed to him so much that we always went home confirmed, strengthened, mellowed, and renewed as children of God.

Jean alone was Bill's nurse, cook, and minister day and night, week after week. Yet despite weariness and stress, she contributed to our gatherings the lightness and warmth of a young fawn on a mountain. Whether she served us high tea or dinner, she made the food appealing and delicious, and more than anyone else, she maintained what Bill wanted— a party spirit that made our meetings fun.

Then there was our minister, George, a loving, self-giving man in his forties, who was never too busy to devote unlimited time to anyone in need. He brought the large gifts of love, Holy Communion, and a sense of the presence of the whole church in our small gathering.

There was Carol, a housewife in her thirties with a gentle face and a sweet, calm spirit. She was our quiet member. From her we learned the beauty and power of the gift of silent presence. She was like a benediction. She sat among us giving love, faithfulness, peace, and courage—sometimes without a word. Pure presence may be closer to the voice of God than the best verbal expression.

There was I, who could be described as a frail looking old lady who was neither frail nor much of a lady. I think I contributed my feeling that death is not a thing of horror but an ordinary part of life, to be dealt with like anything else as best we can. The others found that view steadying.

There was Tom, a brawny twenty-seven-year-old ex-Marine, who was a student at Virginia Theological Seminary. Partly because of clinical training, partly because of a well-remembered illness of his own, and especially because he subordinated himself to the Holy Spirit, he was the sickroom artist of our group. Since his behavior summarizes what is most important in ministering to the sick, I shall focus on how he met needs that usually go unmet.

The diminished vitality of the ill makes them easily

bypassed and momentarily forgotten in group conversations. If you have gathered with others in a hospital to cheer up a sick relative or friend, you know what I mean. When any topic of real interest comes up, the sick person's weak voice commands less attention than the lusty ones. As interest in the subject builds, he or she becomes an outsider, while the visitors talk earnestly with each other. Occasionally, someone turns self-consciously toward the bed. The message of isolation rings out like a tolling bell to the one who is already feeling cut off by illness.

One might think that this could not have happened in our group. It certainly could. We were all deeply committed to our faith, and part of our assignment from Bill was to talk about faith. Caught up in a subject paramount to us all, for long, precious moments we could have failed to focus on Bill. Several times, when I unconsciously edged toward that hidden trap, Tom inconspicuously pulled me back.

In a long illness, the person's physical sensations loom large in his experience. He needs to talk about what fills his time and mind. On the other hand, people who have not undergone long illness understandably prefer not to hear much about it. Yet when friends seem bored, distressed, or a little disapproving—"Try to think about something more pleasant, dear!"—distance is created between sick and healthy persons. If their world of pain, grim facts, and weakness is taboo to their friends, the sick feel unfit for fellowship with normal people.

Upon arrival, Tom always inquired interestedly into details of how Bill was and had been feeling. He never steered Bill back to generalities from specifics. The usual sickroom conversation goes like this:

"How are you feeling, dear?"

"Not too bad. But I do have this funny new pain in my side."

"Sorry to hear that! But in the main you feel better? You look better. Shall I prop you up so you can see the fine day outside?"

This approach only results in sick persons feeling cut off from loved ones. Suffering is their reality. They can't enter the world of fine days until their own world of weariness and pain is shared and understood.

While Tom demonstrated that Bill's world was of interest to one who is well, he also brought his healthy exuberance and vitality with him to Bill's bedside. Good doctors know that health in others is invigorating to those whose vital forces are low. They approach the sick with energy. But many people unconsciously reflect the listlessness they find, even talk in hushed voices, more slowly than usual and with special inflections. This behavior conveys the message that the sick are far separated from the healthy, and it makes the illness the measure of the person's being.

Tom recounted the best of his current experiences to Bill. "I had a totally glorious time Monday," he would begin, his face and voice radiating the remembered pleasure. He would then review in colorful detail what had made Monday special.

People often fear to do this, lest they fill the sick with bitterness and envy. But vicarious participation is close enough to real experience for us all to enjoy stories of triumph, love and adventure. When friends share exciting moments with us, our participation is even more real. The sick, especially, because their own lives are barren, need the extension of their being that healthy friends can give. They need to be talked to and responded to in the same ways they enjoyed when they were well.

Indeed, the sick need the same kinds of relationships that healthy people need. One of the hardest things to bear in a long illness is that our relationships deteriorate along with our health. If our relationships remain intact, sickness has far less power over our hearts.

Physical contact is important to the sick. Illness makes one feel repellent, and hard evidence abounds that one is. Some people are visibly repelled by sickness. Others act as if all illnesses were contagious. Tom acted as if touching Bill was as pleasant as touching healthy persons. He held his hand, hugged him, stretched out beside him on his double bed. He maintained an air of attentive gaiety that made Bill feel interesting, important, attractive, fun to be with, and valued as a friend. He sent the message that Bill was a full-scale person, undiminished by his physical condition.

On our last gathering with Bill, we mostly prayed. Bill's prayers revealed his readiness to meet his Lord. The presence of God was fragrant in the room, and the Holy Spirit moved into Tom, pushed him out, and had his way. I shall always carry behind my eyes the image of Tom lifting with his forefinger from Bill's unhealthy cheek a slowly rolling tear. He brought it to his healthy mouth and said:

"It tastes salty."

Only the Lord does things like that. When we see a man do them, we know that as on the road to Emmaus, the Lord is here.

Don't misunderstand. I know Tom is no better than other men. I know who tasted that tear. That brief gesture spoke more of the acceptance of tears, sickness, and the whole being of Bill than any sonnet could speak. Watching, how could I not know that the Holy One was here, blessing his body, the church?

I cannot share in a death without recalling a November night when I woke suddenly, but softly, at four o'clock to find the glory of the Lord shining round me and the sweetness of the Lord like a warm perfume in the cold room. I heard no sound, yet inside me bells were ringing, "All is well, all is well."

With wonderful certainty, I suddenly knew that the substance which sustains the world is love—on which during life we float in our small boats as on a great fresh lake. I knew that all around us are these living waters. I felt gloriously safe, as when I was very small and crawled into my mother's bed to be snuggled in her arms.

The feeling lasted until eight o'clock, when I got a long distance call. It was my sister. My mother had died that morning—at four o'clock.

I knew then that our Lord had sent her to me, before he called her to slumber or to fulfill whatever tasks he had for her until his day. There was no psychological reason for the experience. I had not expected her death, nor had I been thinking of her often. My consciousness was invaded by the experience as a meteor invades our earth. And I knew with certainty that she loved me, which I had not always believed.

In our foolish humanness, we clutch and cling to earthly life because it is familiar and we shrink from the unknown. But we need not fear to enter a land from which such things as this come, a land from which love comes and to which in time it goes.

DATE DUE

HIGHSMITH 45-220